Highlights in American History:

Its Beginnings to 1850

by Grace Kachaturoff

Professor Emeritus
University of Michigan–Dearborn

illustrated by Ralph Hashoian
Dearborn Public Schools

© Frank Schaffer Publications, Inc.   FS-10143 Highlights in American History–to 1850

FS-10143 Highlights in American History–to 1850
All rights reserved–Printed in the U.S.A.
Copyright © 1994 Frank Schaffer Publications, Inc.
23740 Hawthorne Blvd.
Torrance, CA 90505

TABLE OF CONTENTS

INTRODUCTION

This book is the first of two which focuses on the history of the United States. Part One concentrates on the beginnings of our nation through the 1850s. Part Two treats the events in our nation's history from 1850 to present day. One of the goals of this series is to develop more student interest and enthusiasm in social studies and to bring historical understandings and insights to the existing social studies curriculum. It is the intent of the author for students to respond more positively to the study of history, after having experienced some of the supplementary materials and teaching activities suggested in this publication.

Each unit is highlighted by a short two-page explanatory discussion which emphasizes important ideas of a specific period of time in our history. Successful and productive citizens need a real working knowledge and understanding of the past and the present. Ideas of historical significance are presented to help students gain insights that should be valuable to them as citizens in today's world. This explanation is brief, enriching and reinforcing the discussion in their textbooks, and students should be able to focus on some of the more significant ideas of the era. This is followed by two student activities which attempt to challenge the students to think critically—comprehending, analyzing, synthesizing, and valuing—about the story of our nation. Each unit culminates with a number of suggestions for teaching strategies which teachers may develop for their classrooms which encourage independent and group work and work to be accomplished together cooperatively as a class. Often, data is presented for the teacher which may be shared with the students in developing a particular strategy.

In developing a sense of history and their role in making history, students are encouraged to become involved through various activities and suggested readings, nonfiction and fiction. Students oftentimes enjoy selecting a fiction book about history for relaxation and enjoyment. Some students are motivated to study history after reading historical fiction.

History can help students develop a sense of where things have come from and where they may be heading for and at what speed. The events in our history should be viewed in relationship with other events. These connections or relationships may well be the most significant facts about our historical past. The ideas of historical significance focus on change. Change is the heart of our nation's story and the story of all societies of the world, especially in our era. Through the study of history, students should be encouraged through involvement and thinking, to fit all the parts into a meaningful whole in developing a sense of history and their role.

STUDYING OUR HERITAGE

In studying our heritage, all aspects of the human experience need to be considered, along with the connections between life today and life in the past. It is interesting to know what people have done in the past, so that we might know what we can do in the future. Knowledge of our heritage provides us with the tools for better understanding ourselves and the problems of contemporary society.

The problems of living together in society involve all of the areas of social studies. Political problems cannot be understood in isolation from economic problems nor can they be understood in isolation from their historical backgrounds. The true nature of social studies is the study of human relationships. For purposes of intensive study of various aspects of human relations, social studies are divided into particular areas such as history, economics, government, anthropology, sociology, and a few others. However, a genuine understanding of the nature of human relations can come only through a simultaneous study of all these areas or disciplines.

The story of our heritage is changing. Social scientists write about the past from their own particular points of view and values. They study the available evidence and then they describe it as they see it. They strive to be scholarly and scientific in their descriptions. However, they can only hope that the event occurred in the way they described it. If new evidence is found, the description of the event may change. Lost documents can be found, bones can be unearthed, permission may be given to release personal letters and files, and other types of information may be gathered years after an event. Additional evidence provides social scientists with new insights and new interpretations. Therefore, when more evidence is discovered, the story of people changes.

Since what is read and studied is an interpretation by a specialist, we should be aware of the validity of the evidence that is used and the academic background of the social scientist. It is the responsibility of social scientists to formulate the story of people as clearly and accurately as possible, based on all available evidence. In addition, social scientists should be prepared to defend and to change their interpretations when more evidence is available.

There are endless opportunities for different interpretations of evidence. Social scientists living today are interpreting our heritage from their points of view. Historically, the social studies included stories of important events and great leaders only. It related events about politics and governments; it emphasized the role of rulers and the wars which were waged. Today it is more than that. Social scientists now believe that every aspect of life and ordinary men and women in all types of groups are worthy of study. The experiences of minorities, immigrants, women and families, children and young adults, public health, popular culture, and values are only a few of the themes which are major concerns for social science specialists. A social studies textbook published 30 or 40 years ago would not have included these aspects of human life, but they do today.

Social scientists can be extremely helpful in providing the knowledge necessary for us to understand people from other times and other places. They help to create the story of how people lived on this planet, fought wars, made a living, ruled themselves, worshipped, thought, and died. Studying our heritage can give us hope for a better future. We should be in a better position to make good decisions based upon our knowledge and understanding of our heritage. The story about the founding and development of our nation is complex. However, the episodes which comprise this story are about fascinating characters and exciting events.

WHY SHOULD WE STUDY OUR HERITAGE?

There are people who believe that studying our heritage is simply pleasurable and fun. Some of the stories are very exciting and others are not so exciting. Yet, many individuals seem to have a desire to know about people who lived in the past and who influenced how we live today. Second, it is also believed that knowledge about people, past and present, is a powerful tool to help us make intelligent and rational decisions. To misunderstand and misjudge the events of today may be the result of ignorance of our past. Third, in the study of people in different times and places, we become acquainted with others. We may learn from their experiences. We may also develop empathy for others in our human relationships as we interact in our family, school, and community groups.

Studying about people provides the knowledge and hope that the decisions we make in the future will make a difference. It should help us to develop insights and understandings of where we are and where we are going. Studying our heritage should help us become more perceptive and more thoughtful in coping with experiences in living now.

Do you agree or disagree that studying about people is interesting and enjoyable? Why?

_____
_____
_____
_____

Why do you think it is important to know about the heritage of our nation?

_____
_____
_____
_____
_____
_____
_____

Name _____

STUDYING PEOPLE AND EVENTS

The social scientists study about unusual and fascinating people and exciting events.

1. Prepare a chart listing at least two interesting people you have studied in social studies and then tell why you think they are important and/or influential in the story of our nation.

PERSON	IMPORTANCE/INFLUENCE
1.	
2.	

2. Prepare a chart listing at least two exciting events you studied about in social studies and then tell why you think they are important in the story of our nation.

EVENT	IMPORTANCE
1.	
2.	

3. Optional Activity: Ernest R. May, a Harvard University historian, quotes a Spanish humanist, Juan Louis Vives, in one of his articles:

   "Where there is history, children have transferred to them the advantages of old men; where history is absent, old men are as children."

   What do you think the author of this quotation was saying? Do you agree with him? Why or why not? _____

   _____

WHO ARE THE SOCIAL SCIENTISTS?

Social scientists have the responsibility to help us understand the past and the present of human experience.

Note the responsibility of each social scientist listed below:

Social Scientist	Responsibility
1. Historian	
2. Geographer	
3. Political Scientist	
4. Economist	
5. Sociologist	
6. Anthropologist	
7. Archeologist	

Optional Activity: Select one of the social scientists listed above and find out how one prepares to pursue that field as a career.

THE VOYAGE OF CHANGE

In reality, the land discovery of Columbus in 1492 was an accident. Columbus and his brave sailors were looking for the Far Eastern countries of Asia, the "Indies." Columbus wanted to reach the "Indies" lands from which the Europeans had been getting spices, lovely Oriental rugs, porcelains, and many other luxuries to enrich their lives. In the fifteenth century the Turks overpowered the Europeans and refused to let them use the overland trade routes. About this time, Portuguese sailors discovered that they could sail around the coast of Africa and eventually reach India to continue the trade more cheaply and more safely than by the overland routes.

It depends upon one's point of view as to how to regard the voyages of adventurous Christopher Columbus. We now know that the ancestors of native Americans, thousands of years before his arrival, traveled to this continent through the Bering Straits and continued southward, eventually reaching the southern tip of South America. We also now know that brave Norse fishermen explored the areas around Iceland and Greenland long before Columbus. According to legend, one Norseman, Leif Ericson, became the first European to set foot in North America. Columbus, most likely, was not aware of Leif Ericson and his voyages.

Europeans were looking for ways to continue and expand their trade with the Indies. Sturdier ships were designed to withstand the high ocean waves. The compass and the astrolabe were improved, providing the tools for sailors to tell locations and distances at sea. Europeans were becoming curious about the world in which they lived; they wanted to know more about it. Many theories and maps regarding the size and shape of the world were available. After hundreds of years, Aristotle's idea that the earth was round was again being discussed. European rulers were interested in expanding the power and influence of their new nations through trade and were willing to sponsor courageous sailors to pursue the search for more wealth.

Columbus was born into a humble Italian family. His father was a weaver and at one time he also operated a wine shop. Columbus had little or no formal education. Because of his intense interest in sailing and geography, he learned largely on his own. He believed the world was round, but he did not have any conception of the distances involved. After applying for financial aid to find the "Indies," he finally received a grant from Ferdinand and Isabella, the rulers of Spain. They also bestowed upon him the title of admiral of all the lands and islands which he might find on his voyage.

By August of that year he started off with three small ships and about 100 sailors on a voyage which was to be a momentous event in history. Fortunately, the three ships made passage from the Canary Islands to the Bahamas in about five weeks under clear skies and a steady east wind. Columbus was an able sea commander and an accomplished navigator. In spite of the crew's anxiety at the length of the voyage, Columbus maintained a calm state of mind toward his goal. Finally, at the break of day on October 12, 1492, he sighted land. Surrounded by the awe-stricken natives, Columbus took possession of the land in the name of Ferdinand and Isabella and called it "San Salvador." Returning to Spain, Columbus announced his findings and shared his adventures with many people throughout the European world. In so doing, he made a lasting impression upon the history of the world. Even though he found neither gold nor spices, the Spaniards were happy about his successful voyages.

In actuality, the inhabitants of the land Columbus discovered dated their history at least 15,000 years before his arrival. Their history includes the growth of major urban areas, highly developed agricultural practices, empires, and many other aspects of development that were characteristic of peoples on other continents who were creating their own unique societies.

This discovery brought about interaction among peoples of different continents. People learned from one another. Native Americans were important in developing commerce between the continents. They traded furs for iron pots, blankets, and eventually guns and alcohol. The Europeans developed a taste for new crops such as corn (maize), squash, tomatoes, beans, and potatoes. When the Europeans discovered that the native Americans could not be recruited to work on their plantations, they went to Africa and brought enslaved workers to the New World. Native Americans and Africans bowed subserviently to the technological power, violence, and greed of the Europeans. Even today some native Americans are confined to reservations.

The Europeans, as they founded settlements in the New World, brought their own crops and domesticated animals such as pigs, cows, and horses. The native Americans, also, learned to cultivate European crops and to keep the domesticated animals. The horse became important in some tribal groups, changing traditional ways of hunting and warfare.

Civilization throughout the world was enriched by new crops, furs, gold, horses, and many other things and ideas. This interaction also brought about the enslavement of people, diseases, and racism. Unfortunately, European diseases spread throughout the native American population and millions of people died.

Columbus, during his lifetime, believed that he had reached the "Indies." Nevertheless, he deserves the fame and glory for his accomplishments, which ultimately came to him.

COLUMBUS CROSSES THE OCEAN

Columbus and his sailors crossed the Atlantic Ocean in three ships without encountering any severe storms although the voyage was a fearsome one. After a number of misfortunes such as the wreck of the *Santa Maria* and the desertion of some sailors, he returned to Spain to receive his honors, still not knowing that he failed to reach Asia nor that he had discovered the more wealthy regions of another continent.

1. Why did the sailors believe the voyage was a "fearsome" one? Do you think that astronauts today also sense fear when they are on their missions in outer space? Why or why not? Are there any similarities between Columbus's sailors and astronauts? Why or why not?

   _____

   _____

   _____

2. Why was the discovery of Columbus called "America" and not named after him?

   _____

   _____

   _____

3. On an outline map, show the route taken by the three ships as they made their way to the new world and their return to Spain. What happened to the ships on their return trip? Why not? Also, on the outline map, show the other three voyages made by Columbus.

4. Optional Activity: Write a short composition explaining what the following statement means. The words enclosed by quotation marks were made by John Fiske, United States historian and philosopher.

   The discovery of Columbus in 1492 brought together two hemispheres of our planet and "mingled the two streams of human life which had flowed for countless ages apart."

Some questions to help you in your analysis:
What are the two hemispheres? The two streams of human life?
Do you think the "mingling" of the "two streams of human life" has improved the quality of life on this planet? Why or why not? Explain.

INTERPRETING THE STORY OF COLUMBUS

Social scientists study about people by collecting whatever evidence they can find, studying the evidence thoroughly, and then describing the evidence as they interpret it or as they see it. They decide whether the evidence is important and what it means. Therefore, social scientists may interpret the same event differently. It is the objective of the social scientists, though, to present the story of people as truthfully as they can on the basis of the collected evidence.

The facts remain the same; the changes occur in the interpretation. When new evidence and new insights are developed, previous interpretations may be in error. Therefore, social scientists are constantly re-examining the story of people and trying to present it as accurately as they can. In reading about the heritage of our nation, we need to examine the stories and their interpretations with a critical mind.

Social scientists, as they develop the story of people, try to answer four important questions: What happened? How did it happen? Why did it happen? What are the consequences of what happened?

Using the story about Columbus, answer the following questions:
1. What happened?

_____

_____

2. How did it happen?

_____

_____

3. Why did it happen?

_____

_____

4. What are the consequences of what happened?

_____

_____

Do you think the story about Columbus is the same today as when it was written in 1900? How has it changed? Why?

SUGGESTED TEACHING ACTIVITIES

1. The National Museum of Natural History presented an exhibition in commemoration of Columbus's discovery, entitled *Seeds of Change*. The "seeds," such as corn, sugar, the horse, diseases, and slavery, began changing the way people lived throughout the world, influencing us, even today. Students may be assigned to design a bulletin board illustrating the theme of the exhibition which is discussed in *Seeds of Change* by Herman J. Viola and Carolyn Margolis.

2. Studying Old Maps: Have students bring in copies of old maps such as the Toscanelli Map (1474), the Lenox Globe (1510), Finaeus's Map (1531), Munster's Map (1540), the Mercator's Map (1541), and other available ones. If possible, duplicate the maps for each student and/or project them onto the wall with an overhead projector. Class Discussion: What are the differences between the maps? Why? What do you think of the intelligence of the map makers of that period? Compare those maps with contemporary maps in your classroom. How are they similar? How are they different? Why? On the chalkboard, list the changes that have occurred in map making in the last 100 years.

3. Assign students the role of being sailors on the *Santa Maria*. They will then keep diaries containing at least five entries of their adventures as they leave and sail for the New World. Also, students can assume the roles of the young "Indians" awaiting Columbus and his sailors on the shores of the discovered continent. Have students record their reactions as they see and watch the Europeans for the first time.

4. Have students explain how the following tools, persons, and/or events helped to open the New World for European exploration: Vinland, Leif Ericson, Crusades, astrolabe, compass, trade, *Nina*, Christianity, Marco Polo, Ferdinand and Isabella.

Suggestions for Supplementary Reading:

Dor-Ner, Zvi, and William G. Scheller. *Columbus and the Age of Discovery*. New York: William Morrow and Company, Inc., 1991.

Levinson, Nancy Smiler. *Christopher Columbus: Voyager to the Unknown*. New York: Lodestar Books, 1990.

Matthews, Rupert. *Explorer*. Eyewitness Books. New York: Alfred A. Knopf, 1991.

Simon, Charnan. *Leif Eriksson and the Vikings. The Worlds Greatest Explorers*. Chicago: Children's Press, 1991.

Soule, Gardner. *Christopher Columbus: On the Green Sea of Darkness*. New York: Franklin Watts, 1988.

Viola, Herman J., and Carolyn Margolis. eds. *Seeds of Change: Quincentennial Commemoration*. Washington, D. C.: Smithsonian Institution Press, 1991.

Yue, Charlotte, and David Yue. *Christopher Columbus: How He Did It*. Boston: Houghton Mifflin Company, 1992.

EXPLORATIONS IN THE NEW WORLD

From 1492 until the establishment of the first English settlement at Jamestown in 1607, daring tales of exploration and conquest in the New World occurred. Spaniards landed in Florida looking for the fountain of eternal youth. Some of the explorers—soldiers and noblemen—trekked thousands of miles over the western desert, looking for gold and fabled cities of splendor. Deeply committed missionaries joined the explorers to spread their religious beliefs among the native Americans. During this time the Spaniards, French, and other Europeans were still searching for a route to Asia and its wealth.

John Cabot, an Italian, sailed on behalf of England and reached the mainland of the American continent in 1497. This voyage gave the basis for England's claims to North America. In 1501 Amerigo Vespucci, a passenger on a Portuguese expedition, wrote grandly about all the places he saw in the New World. Many people read the published accounts of his journeys. This led to the naming of the continent after him.

A Portuguese mariner, Ferdinand Magellan, supported by Spanish rulers, set out in 1519 with five ships and about 300 men on a voyage. After touching the Brazilian coast, he and his crew continued sailing to the southernmost tip of South America where they encountered severe storms. Not until they were able to see the Pacific Ocean, about five weeks later, did the storms subside. From that point, they sailed westward for weeks. Magellan had not accurately anticipated the length of the voyage. Without food and water, he and his crew finally reached an inhabited island. Magellan was killed in a fight with the natives on one of the Philippine Islands. Nevertheless, one of his ships, the *Victoria*, continued westward across the Indian Ocean. Then, it rounded the Cape of Good Hope and reached Lisbon in 1522.

This circumnavigation of the globe was significant in many ways. First, it proved that the earth was round. Second, the Europeans now knew that the earth had more water area than land area. Third, it invalidated Columbus's theory that America was a group of islands off the Asiatic coast—a peninsula off the Chinese mainland. The true size and shape of the new continent was not yet developed. Magellan had learned that America was a continent set off by itself and had determined its relationship to the other continents of the world.

As Magellan sailed around the world, the Spaniards were conquering Mexico. In 1519 Hernando Cortes, leading a military expedition with 600 soldiers, set out to find gold and treasures in Mexico. As a smallpox epidemic spread among the natives, the soldiers were able to defeat King Montezuma and the Aztec empire on their second assault. On the ruins of the ancient Aztec capital, the Spaniards built Mexico City in honor of Spain. There were a number of other brutal and savage conquests. Francisco Coronado and Hernando de Soto searched for cities of gold in the southern part of North America. They returned discouraged and disappointed, yet their explorations gave Spain claim to those lands. The Spaniards were gold seekers, not colonizers. The Spaniards governed the American lands and natives with force and very little compassion. Commerce and justice were regulated by Europeans. The native Americans were enslaved politically and spiritually. In spite of these inhumane practices, Spaniards introduced European methods of cultivation, opened gold and silver mines, and built cities, schools, and churches.

Jacques Cartier navigated a ship for the French government, trying to find the water route to China through North America. He sailed with men and women up the St. Lawrence and spent the winter in Montreal. His attempt to establish a French settlement and to find gold, spices, and silks ended without success. On the other hand, the Dutch established the East India Company and set up trading posts at places that are now Albany and New York City.

Since Cabot had not found gold, the English were not interested in the New World. In 1577 Sir Francis Drake, an experienced and daring "sea dog," sailed around the tip of South America and north along the coast of California and claimed those lands for England. More importantly for England, he challenged the Spanish by raiding their ships and taking whatever treasures he found. After the defeat of the Spanish Armada in 1588, the English were considered a powerful force at sea. Now, the English were interested in accumulating wealth and gold.

Sir Humphrey Gilbert and his half-brother Sir Walter Raleigh obtained permission from the English government to claim lands for England which were not in possession of other European countries. Their many expeditions ended in failure. Even a settlement established on Roanoke Island by Sir Raleigh became a "Lost Colony." Sir Raleigh was accused of plotting against the king, imprisoned, and eventually executed in 1618.

The native Americans tried to resist the coming of the Europeans, but they were unsuccessful. Their spears and arrows were no match for the weapons and guns of the Europeans as they pushed westward in the New World.

EXPLORERS AND THEIR ACCOMPLISHMENTS

Match the two columns.

Explorers   Accomplishments

_____ 1. Sir Francis Drake   A. accomplished the first circumnavigation of the earth.

_____ 2. Vasco da Gama   B. established France's claim to territory in the New World.

_____ 3. Christopher Columbus   C. spent a winter in Vinland, located at the northeastern tip of Newfoundland.

_____ 4. Jacques Cartier   D. were probably the first Europeans to reach the New World.

_____ 5. Amerigo Vespucci   E. opened a route to India by sailing around the southern coast of Africa.

_____ 6. Vasco Nunez de Balboa   F. found Florida, giving Spain a foothold in North America.

_____ 7. Vikings   G. established England's claim in North America.

_____ 8. Ponce de Leon   H. explored southwestern North America.

_____ 9. Ferdinand Magellan   I. wrote about the new continent.

_____ 10. Leif Ericson   J. crossed the Isthmus of Panama on foot.

_____ 11. Hernando De Soto   K. made four voyages to the New World.

_____ 12. Francisco Coronado   L. found the Mississippi River.

_____ 13. Hernando Cortes   M. raided Spanish ships and explored the coast of California.

_____ 14. John Cabot   N. conquered the Aztec Empire.

WHAT MAKES A GREAT EXPLORER?

Many men were great explorers during the early exploratory period of North America. John Cabot, Ferdinand Magellan, and others had certain qualities which led them to great adventures in exploration. Today there are also many men and women who have demonstrated their greatness in exploration.

1. What are the three most important characteristics exhibited by the early explorers?

   _____

   _____

   _____

   _____

2. Why were there no women explorers during that period of time?

   _____

   _____

   _____

   _____

3. List at least one male and one female "explorer" of today. They may be doing their "exploring" in space, medicine, public service, the arts, science, social sciences, sports, etc. Describe their accomplishments and tell why they were able to perform as they did.

   _____

   _____

   _____

   _____

4. Have the characteristics needed to be a great explorer changed since the time of Columbus? Explain how and why.

   _____

   _____

   _____

   _____

1. Assign each student to write a script depicting the adventures of explorers. The scripts should be short, from one to three pages. Student guidelines for writing scripts:
   a. Select one interesting and significant event from the adventures of an explorer which is strong in dramatic appeal.
   b. Keep the parts short.
   c. The narrator can provide historical and/or background information that will help listeners fully understand the scene.
   Example form:

   The First Voyage of Columbus

   Narrator: There was much excitement in Europe during the latter part of the fifteenth century. Six new editions of a geography book were published, and the science of navigation was being encouraged by Prince Henry of Portugal. Sturdier ships were being designed, and the compass and the astrolabe were perfected. People were curious and wanted to know about the world. One young man, an outstanding sailor from Genoa, was interested in searching the islands and mainlands in the Atlantic Ocean, possibly reaching the Indies. Let us see what happens as he approaches the king and queen of Spain with his project.

   Columbus: Thank you, your highnesses—King Ferdinand and Queen Isabella—for giving me the honor of an appointment with you. I have come to ask that you aid me in a project that will bring great wealth to you and to Spain.

   King Ferdinand: (His response. . . .)

   Columbus: (His response. . . .)

   Queen Isabella: (Her response. . . .)

   After the scripts are written, an appropriate number of copies should be made for oral dramatizations. The script writer may select students in class to read the roles in front of the class.

2. Topics for further study:
   a. navigational tools, 1400s to 1600s
   b. ships, 1400s to 1600s
   c. Henry Hudson
   d. Aztec Empire
   e. Francisco Pizarro
   f. Sir Humphrey Gilbert
   g. Spanish Armada
   h. Giovanni da Verrazano
   i. Samuel de Champlain
   j. English seadogs

Suggestion for Supplementary Reading:
Morris, Richard B., and Editors of Life. The New World: Prehistory to 1774. vol. 1. New York: Time Inc., 1963.

THE IROQUOIS NATIONS—A CASE STUDY IN CULTURE

When the Europeans first landed on the shores of the American continent, they were overjoyed in anticipation of the wealth to be found. However, they paid little attention to the people occupying the land other than noticing that they were strange and different. They did very little to understand and appreciate the people they found. The early Europeans ignored the native Americans, and when they could not, they fought and killed thousands of them.

The people were erroneously named "Indians" by Columbus. Today, they prefer to be known as "native Americans." In historical context, they will be called "Indians." According to social scientists, the Indians came to this continent originally from Asia thousands of years ago. Hunting and gathering food were their main activities for survival. Some of these people eventually settled around the Great Lakes region and upstate New York about 700 years ago and were known as Woodland Indians. As these Woodland Indians became more acquainted with their environment, they began to change to an agricultural and hunting economy and to identify themselves as the Iroquois.

The estimated population of the Iroquois at one time included about 40,000 people. They lived in rectangular-shaped longhouses, which housed a group of related women and their families. Each family had its own fire for preparing meals. The branches and bark from trees were used to make their longhouses. Also, canoes, farming tools, and household items were made from trees. The maple trees provided sweet syrup.

The men hunted animals such as deer, rabbits, beavers, and foxes with bows and arrows. The animal skins were made into clothing, and the bones were used for making jewelry and small tools. The men fished the many lakes and rivers. Another responsibility of the men was to engage in warfare. The victory rituals were fanatical. War captives were tortured to death. The Iroquois did not believe in open attack as did the Europeans. They surprised their enemies, fought fiercely, and then made a fast retreat. The retreat was not a sign of cowardice but a part of their war making. The attitude of Iroquois warriors toward war was not typical of other Indian groups.

The women managed the household, and they were permitted to divorce their husbands by simply putting their belongings outside the home. The women with their young children raised many varieties of corn, beans, and squash and gathered berries, fruits, nuts, and wild grains. The Iroquois women were powerful, electing the tribal leaders and dismissing leaders if they were displeased with their decisions and behavior.

Usually about 50 to 250 people lived in a compact village. One longhouse in each village was used for group meetings to make plans for protecting the village and getting food. Many religious ceremonies and festivals were also held there. One of them, the Green Corn ceremony, lasted for three days, during which time the Iroquois offered prayers and dances of thanksgiving to the Great Spirit.

The Iroquois engaged in many arts and crafts. They made attractive baskets and were known for their skills in carving false-face masks out of wood. They also used quills and beads to adorn clothing and utensils. Around 1800, when silver became available to them, they made beautiful jewelry. They made lovely wampums to use in their rituals, to commemorate important events, and as symbols of peace. The wampum clamshells were finely shaped and strung together to make belts.

According to legend, Degandawida, a Huron refugee, was sent to the Iroquois in a white canoe by the Great Spirit to communicate a peace plan. Degandawida, in a vision, had seen a huge spruce tree which signified the Iroquoian nations. This tree reached the sky and the land of life with an eagle perched on top, guarding the Iroquois from their enemies. The five roots of the spruce tree were symbolic of the five Iroquois tribes. Hiawatha, a Mohawk chief, developed and organized the Iroquoian Confederacy. The purpose of the confederacy was to promote peace among individuals, among tribes, and to deliberate matters of self-government.

The confederacy included five nations—the Mohawks, Oneidas, Onondagas, Cayugas, and Senecas. During the 1720s the Tuscarora nation was added to this group. This confederacy was viewed as a powerful political group and survived for at least 300 years. No Iroquois tribe was to make war on another, and they lived in peace among themselves for several years. The confederacy consisted of 50 chiefs, but each of the nations only had one vote. Each nation had a council made up of village chiefs, all men. In addition to the regular members of the council, a group called the Pine Tree Chiefs was later formed. These warriors were selected because of their outstanding fighting ability. They participated in the council but had no vote.

The Iroquois were probably better organized than other tribes around them. Although they were warlike and often behaved cruelly, they were compassionate toward friends. Their rituals, legends, and prayers were beautiful and poetic.

STUDYING OTHER AMERICAN INDIANS.

There were many Indian nations throughout America. Prepare a chart showing the way of life of one of the following:

Apache	Crow	Chippewa	Creek	Maya
Nez Perce	Hopi	Seminole	Comanche	Cheyenne
Cherokee	Aztecs	Tlingit	Ottawa	Navajo

Selected Indian Group

History Tell about the nation's beginnings.	
Geography Tell where the people of the nation were located.	
Economy Tell how they made a living and the responsibilities of men and women.	
Government Tell how the leader was chosen and how rules were made.	
Social Organization Tell how people were related to one another.	
Religious Beliefs Tell how they explained the unknown.	
Education Tell how they trained children.	
Artistic Accomplishments Tell about their literature, arts, music, dance, and crafts.	

SHAWNEE CHIEF, A MAN OF PEACE

Read the following famous speech made by Logan, a Shawnee Chief, after he was defeated by the Virginia militia. Earlier, his entire family was slaughtered by settlers led by Thomas and Michael Cresap. Even though the Shawnee Chief was known as a friend of the white settlers, he did, nevertheless, take revenge by having his warriors kill white settlers.

Thomas Jefferson was so impressed with Chief Logan's speech, which he made in his own defense, that he noted it in his 1775 account book (Huntington Library, California).

"I appeal to any white man to say, if ever he entered Logan's cabin hungry, and he gave him not meat: if ever he came cold and naked, and he clothed him not. During the course of the last long and bloody war Logan remained idle in his cabin, an advocate for peace. Such was my love for the whites, that my countrymen pointed as they passed, and said, 'Logan is the friend of white men.' I had even thought to have lived with you, but the injuries of one man. Colonel Cresap, the last spring, in cold blood, and unprovoked, murdered all the relations of Logan, not even sparing my women and children. There runs not a drop of my blood in the veins of any living creature. This called on me for revenge. I have sought it: I have killed many: I have fully glutted my vengeance: for my country I rejoice at the beams of peace. But do not harbour a thought that mine is the joy of fear. Logan never felt fear. He will not turn on his heel to save his life. Who is there to mourn for Logan? Not one."

Answer the following questions:

1. What kind of a person was Chief Logan? Explain why you think so.

_____

_____

_____

2. Do you think he was justified in seeking revenge? Why or why not?

_____

_____

_____

3. Do you think that Chief Logan is a man of peace? Explain.

_____

_____

_____

SUGGESTED TEACHING ACTIVITIES

1. Assign students to write a composition addressing the following questions.
    a. What did the Europeans learn from the Indians?
    b. What did the Indians learn from the Europeans?
    c. How did differing views lead to conflict between the two groups?

2. Assign students to study about the native Americans who lived or are living in their community. Tell about their way of life at the time that Europeans began settling in North America and then note their way of life and how it has changed because of contacts with the settlers.

3. If possible, invite a native American to class to demonstrate a craft and/or to talk about Indian ways of life and how they have changed through time.

4. Check with the Commission on Indian Affairs for your state to get information about any Pow Wows that are scheduled near your community during the school year. Plan a field trip to attend a Pow Wow.

5. Read to the class *Brother Eagle, Sister Sky: A Message from Chief Seattle* by Susan Jeffers (New York: Dial Books, 1991). Show the paintings in the book by Susan Jeffers. Questions for discussion: What does the painter tell us about the beliefs of native Americans regarding nature? Why did the native Americans believe that the earth and the creatures on the earth are a part of human beings? Why should people treat the rivers with kindness? What are some ways that we can make our community aware of the importance of preserving our natural legacy?

6. Have students volunteer to read a trade book about Indians/native Americans and have them share the information they learned with their classmates. A few suggestions:
    Brown, Dee. *Bury My Heart at Wounded Knee: An Indian History of the American West.* New York: Bantam, 1972.
    Hale, Janet Campbell. *The Owl's Song.* New York: Avon, 1976.
    Jones, Weyman. *Edge of Two Worlds.* New York: Yearling Books, 1970.
    O'Dell, Scott. *Sing Down the Moon.* New York: Yearling Books, 1979.
    Sheppard, Sally. *Indians of the Eastern Woodlands.* New York: Franklin Watts, 1975.

Suggestions for Supplementary Reading:
LaFarge, Oliver. *A Pictorial History of the American Indian.* New York: Crown Publishers, Inc., 1956.
Poatgieter, Hermina. *Indian Legacy: Native American Influences on World Life and Culture.*
    New York: Julian Messner, 1981.

EARLY SETTLEMENTS IN THE AMERICAS

The Spaniards built a huge empire in the Americas. Thousands of adventurers and many more thousands of African slaves were brought to their colonial empire in the Americas. The Spanish were a powerful force in the New World. Yet, only a few Spaniards settled in the new colonies to create a self-contained Spanish society. The majority of the population were native Americans and African slaves. The Spanish throne ruled tightly over them in both political and economic matters. A Spanish fort was established in 1565 at St. Augustine, Florida. This eventually became the first permanent European settlement in what is today the United States.

France founded its first permanent settlement in the Americas at Quebec in 1608. The population of Quebec was slow to grow. The French Protestants were excluded from the settlement, and French Catholics did not wish to leave their homes in France.

Sir Walter Raleigh and his cousin, Sir Richard Grenville, were granted permission to recruit men to sail to the New World to establish an English colony. Finally, they found Roanoke Island, off the coast of North Carolina, in 1585. Before Sir Grenville left for England, he antagonized the natives by destroying an Indian village as retaliation for a trivial theft. The colonists, instead of preparing homes and clearing lands for farming, spent most of their time looking for gold and a passage to China. When Sir Francis Drake unexpectedly sailed into Roanoke, all of the settlers boarded his ship to return to England, abandoning the colony.

Sir Raleigh did not give up his dream to establish a colony. In 1587 he recruited 91 men, 17 women, and 9 children to establish a permanent settlement on Roanoke. Shortly after arriving, one of the women gave birth to a daughter, Virginia Dare, the first American-born child of English parents. The ship returned to England to get more supplies and to recruit other settlers. The commander, who had left his family behind, hoped to return in a few months but was unable to do so because of hostilities between Spain and England. When he did return after three years, in 1590, he found the island deserted. He could not find any clues to determine what happened to the settlers, including his own family. Some social scientists believe the settlers were killed by the Indians in revenge for Sir Grenville's retaliation, or perhaps the settlers themselves had developed hostilities with the Indians. Other social scientists think that the settlers could have joined Indian families. To this day, there is no answer to the mystery of the "lost colony."

The incident at Roanoke probably discouraged the English to engage in more explorations, but not for long. Instead of the king of England sponsoring expeditions, the merchants established companies. These trading companies received charters from the king to colonize America. They would take risks and invest in the New World, sponsoring voyages of exploration and developing and managing a colony. The English colonies were basically a business venture and the companies, of course, were interested in profits. The colonists were responsible to the trading company which financed their journey to the New World.

When the English did establish a settlement, they isolated themselves from the Indians and tried to maintain their way of life, adapting English ways to the American environment. The colonists were directly responsible to the company; they had no direct ties to the king in England. Since the company was only interested in the business aspects of colonization, they left the settlers to themselves to develop their own political and social activities. As the population began to increase, they became an American society, not an English society.

The London Company financed an expedition with 144 men which established Jamestown in 1607. The colonists were men, most of whom had not worked for a living. Unfortunately, they selected a poor site covered with thick woods and low and swampy lands for the settlement. The men only wanted to search for gold. They were not interested in building homes and raising food for themselves. Finally, Captain John Smith assumed leadership for the starving and sick colonists. After successfully trading with the Indians for food, he began organizing the settlement. When the men wanted to search for gold instead of farming, he told them if they did not work, they could not eat. Because he was badly burned in an accident, he returned to England for treatment.

Conditions in Jamestown got worse—many people died from diseases and food was scarce. Finally, the settlers decided to abandon the colony. As they were sailing from the settlement, they saw the ships which were bringing them supplies and a new governor. They returned to Jamestown with the supplies and the new governor. From that time on the settlement grew into a permanent one.

Name_____

WHICH EVENT HAPPENED FIRST?

Write the letter of the event that happened first in the blank at the left.

_____1. a. Ponce de Leon arrives on the Florida mainland.
        b. The French government establishes a settlement at Quebec.

_____2. a. Settlers arrive at the Jamestown colony.
        b. Columbus sails west from Spain, searching for Asia.

_____3. a. The Spanish Armada is defeated by the English.
        b. John Cabot establishes the first English claim in North America.

_____4. a. A Spanish fort is built at St. Augustine, Florida.
        b. The settlement at Roanoke is discovered to be a "Lost Colony."

_____5. a. Leif Ericson sets foot in North America.
        b. Christopher Columbus makes his first voyage to the New World.

_____6. a. Ferdinand Magellan's ship, the *Victoria*, reaches Lisbon, after sailing around the world.
        b. Ponce de Leon arrives on the Florida mainland.

_____7. a. Sir Francis Drake sails along the coast of California and claims lands for England.
        b. The settlement at Roanoke is discovered to be a "Lost Colony."

_____8. a. The French government establishes a settlement at Quebec.
        b. The Spanish Armada is defeated by the English.

NATHANIEL BACON'S REBELLION

As a young man, Nathaniel Bacon came to Virginia in 1673 and purchased a farm on the western lands, the frontier, of the colony. Bacon, a member of the governor's council, was prosperous and wanted to extend his ownership of lands. Also, former indentured servants became disgruntled when farm lands were not available to them. They knew there were lands if the colony were extended. The governor, Sir William Berkeley, tried to control colonial expansion to avoid antagonizing the Indians. Sometimes the people living on the frontier felt isolated from the political power based in Jamestown.

Many bloody confrontations between the settlers and Indians occurred in 1676. Bacon and other landholders demanded that the colonial militia be sent to aid them in forcing the Indians to leave. The governor did send the militia, but he ordered them to guard the edge of settlement and not to clash openly with the Indians. Bacon was so angry that he organized his own army and fought the Indians. The governor regarded this act as rebellious and dismissed Bacon from the council.

This incident actually began the revolt against the established authority in the colonies and would culminate in the American Revolution. When the governor called for a new election for members to the House of Burgesses, Bacon became a candidate. He was overwhelmingly elected. The governor was forced to pardon him, promised him a commission to fight the Indians, and restored him to his position on the council. The assembly passed reforms to lessen the authority of the governor.

Later, the governor, thinking that he had undermined Bacon's popular support, again accused Bacon of treason. Bacon then led his army to Jamestown, forcing the governor to flee, and burned the city. Bacon was victorious, but on the verge of his taking command of Virginia, he died of dysentery. The governor regained his control of Virginia.

Answer the following questions:

1. Do you think that Governor Berkeley should have sent out the militia to help Bacon and his army in the conflict with the Indians? Why or why not?

   _____

   _____

2. What is the significance of this incident?

   _____

   _____

   _____

SUGGESTED TEACHING ACTIVITIES

1. Assign two groups of student volunteers to write scripts dramatizing the stories of the "Lost Colony" and Bacon's Rebellion. Duplicate the appropriate number of completed scripts needed, select volunteers for the different roles, and have students read the scripts aloud in class. Students may wish to tape these dramatizations and perhaps play the cassettes for other classes studying American history.

2. Topics for further study:
   - a. Quebec
   - b. Father Marquette
   - c. Sir Walter Raleigh
   - d. House of Burgesses
   - e. St. Augustine
   - f. King James I
   - g. Sir William Grenville
   - h. Sir William Berkeley
   - i. ships (fifteenth century)
   - j. trading companies
   - k. Jamestown
   - l. indentured servants

3. On an outline map of the Western Hemisphere, have students locate the early Spanish, French, and English settlements and identify the European claims in North America in the 1600s. Where were most of the claims located? Why? Which European country had the largest claims? The smallest claims?

4. Have students imagine that they are sailors who returned on the ship from England with the supplies for the colony at Roanoke and discovered that it was deserted. Tell how it felt when they landed and prepared to meet the families who were not there. What did they think happened and why?

5. Have students imagine that they are Indians watching Sir Walter Raleigh's ship approaching their land with settlers. Write a description of the ship, the people who left the ship, and the things they brought with them. Also, have them describe their reactions to the newcomers.

6. Assign students to prepare a chart describing the early settlements: Year of Settlement, Sponsor of Settlement, First Settlers, Location of Settlement, Permanence of Settlement.

7. Have students imagine that they are talk show hosts in London who have as their guests a family who are settlers from Jamestown who are planning to return to the Virginia colony within a few days. Have students list 5 to 10 questions they might like to ask such guests. Then ask for volunteers to assume the role of host or hostess and the members of the colonist family. Enact the interview in class.

8. Have students imagine that they and their families are preparing to leave England to settle in a colony in the New World. List at least 10 things they plan to take with them and tell why they selected them.

ENGLISH SETTLEMENTS IN NEW ENGLAND

The second and more lasting English settlement was established by the Pilgrims in Plymouth. Unlike the colonists who settled in Jamestown, these settlers were determined to make this new land their home. Most of them were Puritans who had broken away or separated themselves from the Church of England, the Anglican Church. They felt there was too much ceremony and ritualism in the Anglican Church. Because of their religious beliefs and practices, they had been imprisoned and persecuted by the English government.

They illegally and quietly left England to settle in the Netherlands. Since they were aliens, they were not permitted to join the guilds so they had to work at difficult jobs for long hours with poor wages. They became concerned that their children were being influenced by the Dutch and that some of them were adopting other religious beliefs. In 1617 the Virginia Company agreed to finance the settlement of about 100 Puritans in Virginia. King James I of England promised them that they could live in the colony with little interference from him.

Finally in 1619 the settlers boarded the *Mayflower* to make the journey to the New World. Cape Cod was sighted in 1620 but the settlers had planned to sail more south. Miles Standish and a few men got off the ship, explored the area, and decided that the land appeared to be suitable for settlement. They decided to make their new homes on an abandoned Indian cornfield.

Because the settlers included Puritans and non-Puritans, the Mayflower Compact was signed which guaranteed that everyone would be treated with justice and equality under the law. The winter in Massachusetts was miserable; it was cold and there was much illness. They met Samoset, an Indian, who spoke a little English which he had learned from English fishermen in Maine. He told the settlers that he had a friend, Squanto, who had been in England and spoke English. Also, Samoset made arrangements for Chief Massasoit to visit, and the settlers signed a peace treaty with him. Because his own family and tribe had died in the smallpox epidemic, Squanto joined the Pilgrims. The Indians were friendly. They taught the settlers how to fish and how to plant corn, peas, and other vegetables. After the harvest, the settlers and the Indians celebrated the first Thanksgiving together.

The colonists elected William Bradford as their governor, and he served for many years with little control from England. When the Puritans had sailed from England, they had agreed with the trading company to share in the profits at the end of seven years. Governor Bradford distributed the communal lands among the families. The colonists were unable to make enough profits from farming to repay the trading company. Later, Governor Bradford and other merchants, from the profits in their fur trading businesses, paid off the company.

In 1630 nearly a thousand emigrants arrived in Boston harbor, financed by the Massachusetts Bay Company. These colonists wanted to worship without the ritualism of the Anglican Church. John Winthrop served as governor and John Cotton as a scholar and preacher. To participate in government, a man had to be a member of a church. Other settlers could live in the colony, but they had to contribute to the support of the Puritan Church and submit to its control in both public and private life.

With so many colonists in the New World, it somewhat relieved them of immediate fear of attacks by the Indians. The colonists were also able to control the settlements on the Massachusetts lands, and finally it led to representative government. The towns demanded, and got, the privilege of sending their own elected representatives to help in the making of laws.

Roger Williams, a minister in Salem, believed in ideas that were not acceptable to the Puritans. He believed that the land belonged to the Indians and that the government should not control the religious ideas of people. He was finally driven from the colony in 1636. He purchased some land from the Indians and began a settlement which he called "Providence." Other dissenters followed Williams, and in 1643 he secured recognition for his colony from the English parliament. The colony of Rhode Island and Providence Plantations provided democracy and religious freedom. Election by ballot was introduced and the colony was governed by all of the free inhabitants.

Anne Hutchinson, an intelligent and strong-minded woman, challenged the beliefs of the Puritans. She believed that divine truths could be revealed directly to the individual, without assistance of minister or church. In 1638 she was convicted and banished from the colony for her beliefs. With her family and some of her followers, she settled on Narragansett Bay in Rhode Island and founded the town of Portsmouth.

Thomas Hooker, a minister, set out with emigrants and all their belongings to establish colonies in Connecticut, where the land was said to be more fertile. He wanted every man, regardless of religious preference, to have the right to vote. In 1639 these colonists wrote the first constitution drawn up in America. They did not require that a man be a member of a church to vote. The clergy had less authority in Connecticut than in any other colony.

Other settlements were established in New Hampshire and Maine. Representative government was achieving a stronghold among the colonists, and the idea of freedom of religion was slowly becoming accepted in the colonies.

IMPORTANT PEOPLE AND IDEAS

Match Column I with Column II.

Column I	Column II

_____1.   Separatists

A.   The settlers, under his leadership, wrote the first constitution in America.

_____2.   Charter

B.   The Pilgrims sailed from England on this ship.

_____3.   Anne Hutchinson

C.   An agreement to form a government and to obey its laws

_____4.   Separation of church and state

D.   They separated from the Church of England because they believed that the Church had fallen away from God.

_____5.   Pilgrims

E.   He believed that religion was a private matter in which government should not interfere.

_____6.   *Mayflower*

F.   A colony established by Roger Williams in Rhode Island

_____7.   Mayflower Compact

G.   She was banished from the Massachusetts Bay Colony for her religious beliefs.

_____8.   Thomas Hooker

H.   The first governor of Massachusetts Bay Colony

_____9.   John Winthrop

I.   An official document that gave certain rights and privileges to a person or group

_____10.   William Bradford

J.   Puritans who left the Anglican Church and were looking for another home

_____11.   Roger Williams

K.   Governor of Plymouth colony for 30 years

_____12.   Providence

L.   A document stating that government should have no authority over religious matters, and the church should have no authority over governmental matters

IDENTIFYING THE NEW ENGLAND COLONIES

1. On another sheet of paper, draw an outline map of New England and show where the colonies founded in the 1600s are located.

2. Provide the following information about one of the colonies founded in New England.

Name of Colony: _____

Year Founded: _____

Why was the colony founded? _____
_____

Who were the people that settled in the colony?_____
_____

Who were the leaders of the colony? _____
_____

What kind of government did they form? _____
_____

What religious beliefs and practices did they observe?_____
_____
_____

What were their relationships with the Indians? _____
_____
_____
_____

1. Assign students to read "English Settlements in New England." A class discussion may involve the following questions:
   - Why were the New England colonies more successful than the colony established in Jamestown?
   - Why did the English wish to come to the New World?
   - Why was a representative type of government established in the colonies rather than a type resembling the one in England?
   - Why were Roger Williams and Anne Hutchinson banished from the Massachusetts Bay Colony? How do you think they brought about freedom of religion?

2. Assign volunteer students to create a time line, showing the period of colonization in New England. For each event have students note the date on a 5 1/2" by 8" index card, create an illustration (cartoon or drawing), and write one brief sentence explaining the event. Then, hang the cards in chronological order on a string in the classroom. More cards can be added during the study of U.S. history.

3. Topics for further study:
   a. Anne Hutchinson
   b. Roger Williams
   c. Squanto
   d. Miles Standish
   e. *Speedwell*
   f. Plymouth Plantation
   g. representative government
   h. Reverend Thomas Hooker
   i. Fundamental Orders of Connecticut
   j. Separatists
   k. John Winthrop
   l. indenture system
   m. smallpox epidemic

4. Have students role play being members of one of the colonies in New England. They will keep a diary of at least three weeks, one entry per week, of their experiences which may include church going, attendance at a town meeting, working on the farm, socializing with other colonists, learning to read, working, and playing.

Suggestions for Supplementary Reading:

Fleming, Thomas J. *One Small Candle: The Pilgrims' First Year in America*. New York: W. W. Norton & Company, Inc., 1964.

Wright, Louis B., and Editors of *American Heritage*. *The American Heritage History of the Thirteen Colonies*. New York: American Heritage Publishing Co., 1967.

MORE ENGLISH SETTLEMENTS IN THE NEW WORLD

In 1632 George Calvert (Lord Baltimore), a Roman Catholic nobleman, obtained a charter from Charles I to establish the Maryland colony as a place of refuge for persecuted Roman Catholics. The colonists were to enjoy all the privileges and liberties of English subjects, no taxes were to be levied by the king, and the laws were to be enacted by the proprietor with the advice of the free men of the colony. George Calvert died before he was able to fulfill his plans but his son, Cecilius Calvert, sent settlers in 1634 to St. Marys, on the shores of Chesapeake Bay. The Calvert family had invested greatly in the colony and wanted profits from this venture. Not many Roman Catholics were attracted to the colony; therefore, the Calverts encouraged anyone to come. The Roman Catholics were a minority. There were many conflicts between people of different religious beliefs. Therefore, in 1649 the famous Toleration Act was passed which provided freedom of worship to all Christians.

England was having difficulties at home. In 1642 the English Civil War began between the supporters of Charles I and the Roundheads. The Roundheads were members of Parliament who were Puritans. In 1649 the Roundheads defeated the forces of Charles I, and they beheaded him. Oliver Cromwell became the protector of England for nine years. After Cromwell's death, the son of King Charles I, King Charles II, returned from exile and regained the throne for the Stuart family. King Charles II rewarded his loyal followers by granting them charters for four additional colonies—Carolina, New York, New Jersey, and Pennsylvania. These colonies were founded as proprietorships, similar to the Maryland colony. The proprietor was given the authority (governing rights) by the king for that colony. Most proprietors never traveled to the colonies they founded. They were primarily interested in profits as landlords and in land speculations. The proprietor was powerful; he could appoint governors, sell land, establish courts, and collect taxes. Generally, there was little interference from the king once the charter was granted.

In 1670 settlers sent out by the proprietors of the Carolina colony (named after Charles II), established a settlement in Port Royal. Ten years later they founded the city of Charles Town, which eventually became Charleston. The Earl of Shaftesbury wanted to plan a well-organized community. However, the plan was not successful. Their charter guaranteed religious freedom to all Christians. The proprietors promised political freedom; laws were to be enacted by a representative assembly. The northern and southern regions of the colony remained separated, largely because of geographical differences. The northern settlers were mainly farmers. In the south the fertile lands promoted a more prosperous economy with large plantations. After Lord Shaftesbury died, the settlers seized control of the colony in 1719. Ten years later, the King of England divided the colonies into North Carolina and South Carolina.

The colony established in Georgia was founded by General James Oglethorpe, a war hero, who wanted to create a military barrier against the Spaniards on the southern border and a haven for debtors. General Oglethorpe, who had investigated the English prisons, believed that many of the honest, imprisoned debtors could become farmers and soldiers in a new colony. He was granted a charter in 1732 to develop colonies in Georgia. Free blacks or slaves and Roman Catholics were excluded from settling in the colony. Indian trade was regulated. Only a few debtors came, but many tradesmen and artisans and other religious refugees arrived in Georgia. Large numbers were not attracted to this colony because of the restrictions. Later these restrictions were repealed or eliminated, and the colony began to increase in population.

In the early 1620s the Dutch established New Amsterdam on the island of Manhattan. Peter Minuit, director of the Dutch West India Company, had purchased, in 1626, Manhattan Island from the Indians for 60 guilders' (24 dollars) worth of trinkets. Not many people wished to leave their homeland to settle in the new colony; therefore, the population grew slowly. In 1647 Peter Stuyvesant, a strong and arrogant leader, was commissioned as director-general of New Netherland. The English, who surrounded this settlement, were envious and wanted the Dutch lands. In 1664 English ships appeared in the harbor of New Amsterdam. Governor Peter Stuyvesant was eager to challenge the English in spite of his peg leg and said that he would rather be carried out dead than surrender. Nevertheless, the Dutch surrendered. New Netherland became an English possession and the Duke of York was made proprietor, renaming the colony New York. Peter Stuyvesant, although bitter because of the surrender, remained in New York until his death in 1672. The land east of the Delaware River was granted to two English nobles who gave their colony the name of New Jersey.

William Penn, an educated young man, had joined the Quakers who believed that they should do what their consciences told them was right. They had no church government or buildings and no clergy; they treated women equally, refused to take oaths and to fight in wars. William Penn was imprisoned for teaching what he believed. After he was released, he was eager to start a colony in the New World where Quakers would not be persecuted. His father was an admiral of the Royal Navy and a landlord of valuable estates. When his father died, he inherited his properties and his father's claim to a large debt from the king. Charles I repaid this debt by granting William Penn a charter to the land between New York and Maryland, to be known as Pennsylvania. He and the Quakers arrived in Pennsylvania in 1682 and founded the city of brotherly love, Philadelphia. Since he believed that the land belonged to the Indians, he purchased it from them. People of all religious beliefs were welcomed to this colony.

VERTICAL TIME LINE

Complete the following time line. Identify each one of the dates with the correct letter from the following events. Then write a sentence which provides more information about the event.

Events:
    a. The Dutch established a settlement on the island of Manhattan.
    b. A settlement was established in Port Royal.
    c. The city of Philadelphia was founded by William Penn.
    d. Peter Minuit purchased the island of Manhattan from the Indians.
    e. Lord Baltimore obtained a charter to establish a refuge for persecuted Roman Catholics.
    f. The Toleration Act was passed.
    g. The Puritans established Massachusetts Bay colony at Boston.
    h. General Oglethorpe was granted a charter to colonize Georgia.
    i. The Dutch surrendered New Netherland to the English.
    j. Jamestown was founded.
    k. The Pilgrims founded Plymouth colony.
    l. The English Civil War began.

YEAR	EVENT	MORE INFORMATION ABOUT EVENT
1607	_____	_____
1620	_____	_____
1620	_____	_____
1626	_____	_____
1630	_____	_____
1632	_____	_____
1642	_____	_____
1649	_____	_____
1664	_____	_____
1682	_____	_____
1732	_____	_____

COLONIAL POPULATION GROWTH

The estimated population figures show the beginnings of a pattern of growth which eventually led the white settlers to outnumber the native population. The white population not only included English men and women but also other Europeans. Free English laborers, businessmen, artisans, and religious dissenters found their way to America. Many individuals came as indentured servants who worked out a term of servitude, usually from four to five years, to repay the monies for their passage, food, and shelter.

Prepare a bar graph showing the following information.

Colonial Population Estimates (in round numbers)					
Year	Population	Year	Population	Year	Population
1610	350	1660	75,100	1710	331,700
1620	2,300	1670	111,900	1720	446,200
1630	4,600	1680	151,500	1730	629,400
1640	26,600	1690	210,400		
1650	50,400	1700	250,900		

What does your graph tell about colonial population growth? What factors may contribute to population growth?

SUGGESTED TEACHING ACTIVITIES

1. Topics for further study:
   a. William Penn
   b. indentured servants
   c. General Oglethorpe
   d. Lord Baltimore
   e. Peter Minuit
   f. Peter Stuyvesant
   g. King Charles II
   h. Oliver Cromwell
   i. Roundheads
   j. King Charles I
   k. proprietors
   l. Quakers

2. Assign students to locate the Middle and Southern colonies on an outline map of the United States' eastern coast. Class discussion: Why did the colonists tend to settle on the coastline of America?

3. Assign students to read "More English Settlements in the New World." Then, assign them to prepare a chart about one of the colonies which contains the following information:
   Name of Colony and Year Founded
   Why was the colony founded?
   Who were the people that settled in the colony?
   Who were the leaders of the colony?
   What kind of government did they form?
   What religious beliefs and practices did they observe?
   What were their relationships with the Indians?
   How did the colonists make their living?

4. Assign students to identify one of the leaders or settlers in the colonies to interpret. Some suggestions are William Penn, a Roman Catholic colonist in Georgia, a Quaker teen-ager in Philadelphia, or Peter Minuit. Assignment for students: Pretend that you are the individual and prepare a 10-minute monologue telling about yourself, your work, and your ideas to your classmates. When you are making the presentation, make an effort to dress accordingly, to create the proper environment, and to use the speech of the period, if possible. Information about the individual can be obtained through reading biographies, autobiographies, and other books and materials.

5. If possible plan a trip to a historical museum to view artifacts from the 1600s and 1700s that tell about the beginnings of our country. Perhaps a student or a parent may be invited to speak to the class about visitations to museums such as Sturbridge Village or Greenfield Village.

Suggestions for Supplementary Reading:

Dolson, Hildegarde. *William Penn. Quaker Hero*. New York: Random House, 1961.
Alderman, Clifford Lindsey. *The Story of the Thirteen Colonies*. New York: Random House, 1966.

THE COLONIAL ECONOMY

In the colonial towns and villages, many craftsmen and artisans established themselves as cobblers, blacksmiths, riflemakers, cabinetmakers, printers, and silversmiths. The major economic activity or means of livelihood, though, was agriculture. At least four-fifths of the colonists were farmers. However, the type of farming practiced in different colonies was varied and quite different depending on the geographical environment.

In the North the conditions for farming were not as favorable as in the South. The land was not as fertile. Farms in most of New England were small. Everyone in the family worked together to grow food and raise animals to make a living. They tried to be self-sufficient. They were able to grow surplus apples and corn and raise livestock to trade with others for things which they could not produce for themselves. The land was more fertile in the middle colonies. Colonial farmers in New York and Pennsylvania were able to grow more fruits and vegetables and raise more livestock which could be sold. They were able to sell wheat to England. Other cereals and potatoes were also grown. As in New England, the farms were small; generally the work was done by the farmer, his wife, and his children.

There was an attempt to develop industries such as the ironworks in Saugus, located near Boston. The ironworks employed several hundred laborers. Water power was harnessed, small mills were developed for grinding grain, others for processing cloth, and some for milling lumber. Large-scale shipbuilding operations began to develop near the harbors. Men did carpentry. Women were involved in spinning, weaving, making clothing, butter, soap, candles, and other tasks basic to the life of the family.

There was very little industrial growth because restrictions were imposed by the English government on metal processing, manufacturing of woolens, and hats. The supply of labor and domestic markets was inadequate. Transportation facilities were also inadequate to transport products from one place to another.

Natural resources such as furs and lumber were exploited by the colonists. As the supply of fur-bearing animals dwindled, fur trading diminished. Large-scale lumbering brought about the disappearance of large forests. Fishing and whaling were pursued by colonists off the shores of New England. These economic activities provided the colonists with commodities which could be exported to England in exchange for manufactured goods which they needed.

In the South agriculture developed in quite a different way. The landholdings of a farmer or planter were vast in acreage. The planter specialized in growing one crop for exporting, not for subsistence. The tobacco plant, in 1614, was brought to Virginia and grown to the exclusion of any other crops. Sir Walter Raleigh first introduced England to smoking. The habit of smoking tobacco spread and became popular among the English even though King James I tried to stop it. The planters prospered by exporting tobacco to England. The cultivation of tobacco required many laborers. The importation of slave labor from western Africa provided the needed workers.

Some parts of the South were not suitable for tobacco growing. In those parts the planters specialized in growing rice. This was difficult work. Again, the planters used slave labor to perform the task. Another crop which was developed in South Carolina was indigo, a source of blue dye. There was great demand for this product in Europe. Cotton was grown, but it did not become a major plantation crop until the very late 1790s. The planters had to rely upon trade with England to make a prosperous living. Smaller industries and crafts were not developed to the same degree in the South as in the North. The South depended upon a single-crop economy based on large land holdings and black slaves. The owners of these vast plantations exerted great power in the government of the South.

The colonists did not have an accepted medium of exchange and in most cases relied upon bartering, the exchange of goods for other goods. Eventually they issued their own paper money. Nevertheless, there was trade among the colonies and between America and England. The colonial workers, although inadequate in numbers, were prosperous and inventive, and there was still a limitless supply of land. Gradually, a middle class of merchants was emerging in an expanding economy.

By the 1600s most of the colonies, founded by proprietors, became royal provinces as the king saw the profits that might be generated for England by controlling trade and manufacturing in the colonies. The "mercantile theory" demanded that a nation try to buy as little from others and sell as much to others as possible. This would create a "favorable balance" for a nation. England saw the colonies as a place to sell goods and as a place which would provide them with raw materials such as furs, wools and iron.

In the 1600s the Navigation Acts were imposed upon the colonists which provided that no goods could be transported into or out of the colonies except by English-built ships with a majority of English crew members. There were many other restrictions which were passed, limiting and controlling trade and manufacturing in the colonies. Many of these restrictions were ignored when the attentions of England were involved in other concerns and conflicts in Europe rather than in the colonies. The colonists sometimes engaged in smuggling and learned that they did not have to obey English laws.

"TRIANGULAR" TRADE—RUM, SLAVES, AND SUGAR

The economy of the South was dependent on having an adequate work force. Workers were needed in the fields to plant and harvest tobacco, rice, and eventually cotton. The growing season in the South was long, hot, and humid; and many manual tasks were required. The colonists found that African black slaves were cheap and relatively immune to tropical diseases.

Intricate and complex systems of coastal trade were developed which provided the colonies with sugar, molasses, and slaves. The ships from New England carried rum and other goods to Africa. They exchanged these products for slaves who were taken to the West Indies. They exchanged the slaves for sugar and molasses which they shipped back to New England to be distilled into rum. The profits from this trade helped the colonists purchase manufactured goods they needed from England and Europe.

Bringing African slaves to the United States occurred during a relatively short period of time. About one-third of the total number of slaves arrived before 1760. The United States government abolished the importation of African slaves in 1808, although some were brought in illegally for a few years afterwards.

Draw an outline map including the eastern American coast, Atlantic Ocean, and the western coasts of Europe and Africa. Identify on the map, by using arrows, the overseas trade routes during the colonial period.

1. List the products which were sent from the Northern colonies to England.
2. List the products sent to Northern and Southern colonies from England.
3. List the products which were sent from the Southern colonies to England.
4. List the products which were sent to West Africa from the Northern colonies.
5. List the products which were sent to the Northern colonies from the West Indies.
6. List what was sent to the West Indies from West Africa.

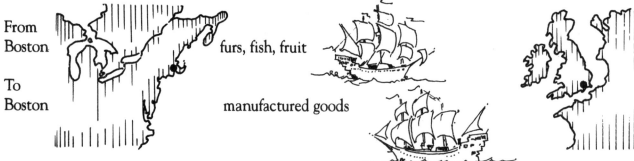

From
Boston   furs, fish, fruit

To
Boston   manufactured goods

COMPARING COLONIAL ECONOMY IN THE NORTH AND IN THE SOUTH

Prepare a chart comparing and contrasting the colonial economy in the North and in the South.

	NORTH COLONIES	SOUTH COLONIES
History		
Geography		
People		
Farm Size		
Crops		
Industries		
Work Force		
Exports		
Imports		

SUGGESTED TEACHING ACTIVITIES

1. Assign students to write a sentence or two telling how each of the following terms influenced the economy in the colonies.

a.	mercantilism	f.	barter	k.	royal colony	p.	rice
b.	subsistence farming	g.	indigo	l.	lumbering	q.	slaves
c.	manufactured goods	h.	corn	m.	self-sufficient	r.	rum
d.	medium of exchange	i.	wheat	n.	fur trading	s.	tobacco
e.	shipbuilding	j.	molasses	o.	fishing/whaling		

2. Assign students to make a chart that compares and contrasts life in New England during the early 1700s with modern family life in the 1900s. Compare family size; responsibilities of father, mother, and teen-agers; jobs; and food.

3. Assign students the role of just having come to one of the colonies in America. The colony may be located either in the North or in the South. Have them keep a diary for five weeks—at least one entry each week—describing their new home and farm, their new life style, people they meet, and the things they see.

4. The colonists tried to be self-sufficient. They made their own cloth and clothing, butter, furniture, toys, barrels, quilts, farm implements, soap, shoes, and many other things. Have students select one of the crafts and be prepared to explain how it was made. (Students may work in groups.) If possible, they should be encouraged to demonstrate how it was made and perhaps even show illustrations and diagrams.

5. If possible, visit a museum in your community which highlights life in colonial times. Have students observe the various crafts made by the colonists. As a class, prepare a list of responsibilities reserved for men, for women, and for teen-agers on the chalkboard. List those responsibilities which are shared. Discuss how these responsibilities compare to the responsibilities that teen-agers have today.

6. Assign student volunteers to create a class mural which depicts the economic life—farming, crafts, trade, industries—for the colonies in the North and in the South.

7. Assign student volunteers to report on the implements used in farming and on the plantations and the equipment used by the printers, silvermakers, cobblers, and other artisans. If possible, show illustrations, simulations, photographs, and/or drawings of the implements and/or equipment.

Suggestion for Supplementary Reading:
Tunis, Edwin. *Colonial Living*. New York: Thomas Y. Crowell, 1957.

LIFE IN COLONIAL AMERICA

Life in colonial America was somewhat different from life in English society. The people in America represented particular interests. Some of them were religious dissenters, others were adventurers, and some were seeking better economic opportunities. The geographical environment in the colonies was different from the homeland so that the English customs and practices could not be continued. Land was plentiful in America, but people and workers were scarce. English people did dominate the population. Some people, though, came from other European nations. A new American culture was evolving and the English culture was being adapted rather than duplicated.

In the South the plantations were relatively small estates. Most landowners lived in rough cabins or simple houses with their servants or slaves nearby. They did not live in luxury and splendor. The plantations were located far from towns so they tended to be self-contained communities. The plantation included the home of the planter, service buildings, barns, and the cabins of the slaves. If the landholders were wealthy, there may have been a school for white children only and a chapel. Since slaves were plentiful, the wives of the owners spent more time with their families as servants performed many of the household tasks. The large landowners were socially and politically in control, not only over the black population on their plantations but also over the usually poor, independent farmers who worked small plots of land.

The black slaves began to develop a culture of their own. About 75 percent of them lived in plantations of 50 slaves or more. They developed a strong and stable family structure in spite of many difficulties. Black women had to care for their families and work in the fields. Some plantations did train slaves in trades and crafts. The black slaves developed language patterns of their own. "Gullah," a combination of English and African languages, was spoken in South Carolina. A distinctive black religion was emerging which blended Christianity with African beliefs and folklore. In some cases the blacks were treated humanely and with justice and other times with cruelty. They were, in all cases, powerless. Some of the blacks rebelled by running away. There were some organized revolts against their masters, but they were quickly crushed.

The Puritan community in the North was different from the plantation community. More people lived in towns. In their small homes, they had a gathering room with a fireplace which was kept going all of the time. They ate, studied, worked, and even slept there. To work and to live together, they drew up covenants, agreements among the members of the community, which bound them together with common goals for unity and harmony. Town meetings were held to solve common problems and to develop a tightly knit community.

The family was an important unit over which the father had great control. Fathers taught their sons how to farm, build homes, and fish. When a young man wished to marry, he asked his parents for permission. When the father died, the lands were divided among all the sons. As the plots of farm land became smaller, many young men decided to seek lands on the western frontier. The mothers taught the daughters how to care for the family, sew, cook, weave, and do other household tasks. Children gathered firewood and helped in preparing peas and corn for cooking and storing. They had little time for play although the girls had dolls and the boys played horseshoes, shot marbles, and spun their tops. Sometimes, they were able to go ice skating and sledding during the winter and attend social gatherings such as barn raisings, quilting bees, and corn huskings.

The colonists believed that education was important. Children were taught by their parents to read and write at home. In 1647 a law in Massachusetts required every town to support a public school by hiring a teacher for every 50 families. Some public schools were established because of this law. Religious groups such as the Quakers established church schools. *Dame schools* were held in the homes of widows or single women to teach children how to read and write.

Boys were taught trades by being apprenticed to a master tradesman for a period of time, usually from four to seven years, or until they were 21 years old. A legal agreement for the apprenticeship was made between the parents and the skilled workers. The apprentice lived in the home of a skilled worker such as a silvermaker, a printer, or a cobbler and was taught the trade. The young apprentice was to be obedient and hardworking. In some towns, schools were established for apprentices to attend during the evening.

Over 50 percent of American boys could read and write. Educational opportunities for girls, Indians, and blacks were not common in the colonies. Primary education in the home was often provided for the daughters as well as for sons. Black slaves were not taught, although a few planters did teach slaves to read and write. The first American college, Harvard University, was founded in 1636 to train ministers and to "advance learning." Five other colleges were founded by 1760. Wealthy white sons usually attended college.

A distinctive colonial vocabulary was developing which included words borrowed from the Indians, black slaves, and the Dutch. Some English words and expressions were changed slightly to accommodate the new environment. A different accent emerged and different dialects developed, reflecting the diversity and expansiveness of the American communities.

Benjamin Franklin was probably the most significant author during the colonial period other than a few ministers. Not many colonists were engaged in writing literature. However, an interest in scientific knowledge was developing; the colonists were beginning to accept the importance of science and reasoning. People were beginning to question their beliefs and ideas. They were able to control and manage their own political affairs. No doubt, they could manage their own social affairs, too.

WITCHCRAFT IN THE COLONIES

In the 1680s and 1690s there was reaction to the many changes which were taking place in the New England colonies. Young men were moving from the established towns to settle in more remote places on the frontier. There were many disputes and conflicts caused by leaving one's town and forming new churches.

The Puritans believed that certain people who possessed mystic powers were witches. These extraordinary powers permitted a "witch" to possess another individual for evil purposes. In Salem, Massachusetts, several girls behaved strangely, having fits, falling, and screaming. They accused "witches" for their behavior. Two West Indian slaves who practiced their superstitious beliefs were accused of witchcraft. Innocent people were unjustly accused of witchcraft. Puritan ministers made untrue accusations to frighten their parishioners into upholding the laws of the church. The accused were often tortured into "confessing" their crimes.

When these unfair trials ended, about 150 persons were tried and 19 of them were publicly put to death in a cruel manner. Most of the false accusations were directed toward young girls and against older women although men were sometimes accused.

Some social scientists believe that the witch trials were the outcome of the changes that New England Puritans were experiencing in their homes, churches, and communities. The Puritans reacted to these changes with fear and guilt and looked for scapegoats which they found by accusing persons of witchcraft.

1. Why do you think the Puritan ministers generally supported the trials for witchcraft?

   _____

   _____

2. Do you think that the social scientists are justified in believing that the Puritans were merely looking for scapegoats during this time in their history? Do you think we sometimes look for scapegoats when there is a problem in our society today? Explain. _____

   _____

   _____

3. Optional: Some social scientists believe that a moldy grain growing in the fields around Salem could have caused the girls to behave strangely. Try to find some information to support or refute this statement.

COMPARING LIFE IN THE NORTH AND IN THE SOUTH

Make a chart comparing life on a farm in New England and life on a plantation in the South.

	Life on a Farm	Life on a Plantation
Family		
Home		
Clothing		
Religion		
Farming		
Education		
Government		
Use of Black Slaves		
Recreational Activities		

SUGGESTED TEACHING ACTIVITIES

1. Topics for further study:
   a. Harvard University
   b. Yale University
   c. Princeton University
   d. Columbia University
   e. University of Pennsylvania
   f. apprenticeship
   g. Benjamin Franklin
   h. covenants
   i. witchcraft
   j. *The Crucible* by Arthur Miller

2. Have students study the contributions of women in colonial life. What role do you think women played in the development and growth of American society? On the chalkboard, list the ways in which a woman's life in colonial times differs from a woman's life in today's society.

3. Assign students to find out what games colonial children and young people played. If possible, have student volunteers explain how to play a game and then have everyone in the class participate. Discuss as a class how games differ from games played today.

4. Assign students to plan the menu for a New England family and a family on a southern plantation for one day. What are the most available foods? How are they prepared? Some students, perhaps with the help of the home economics teacher, may wish to volunteer to prepare a booklet of colonial recipes and perhaps plan a meal for the entire class which may have been served in a New England home or on a southern plantation.

5. If a child were born into a New England family, what names might the parents consider for a son? A daughter? Why were these names often used by parents in naming their children?

6. Assign students to select one of the crafts practiced by the colonists and then to demonstrate, if possible, the craft for their classmates. Some of the crafts may be candlemaking, butter making, cheese making, drying fruit, weaving, spinning, making cider, or making toys.

7. Have students list the different career options which were open for young ladies and for young men during the colonial times. Are these options still open today? Why or why not?

Suggestions for Supplementary Reading:

Smith, Carter, ed. *Daily Life: A Sourcebook on Colonial America*. American Albums from the collections of The Library of Congress. Brookfield, Connecticut: The Millbrook Press, 1991.

Tunis, Edwin. *Colonial Living*. New York: Thomas Y. Crowell, 1957.

RIVALRY BETWEEN FRANCE AND ENGLAND IN THE NEW WORLD

Being a part of the British Empire gave the early Americans many benefits. The mother country provided the colonies with military protection and opportunities for trade and commerce. England attempted to regulate trade in the colonies but more or less left the colonists alone. The colonists were, therefore, able to develop representative government and political stability. The relationship between the colonists and the English government was good. However, as the British government gained dominance in world power, its policies toward the 13 colonies changed.

Beginning in 1689 the British and the French were competing for world power. In 1754 the colonists were threatened by the French. Representatives from certain colonies met in Albany to negotiate a treaty with the Iroquois Indians. They also drew up the Albany Plan, prepared by Benjamin Franklin, to provide for mutual defense. However, none of the colonies approved this plan.

By 1750 the English and French settlements in North America had expanded, creating conflicts and tensions between them. There were probably about 1,500,000 English settlers in the colonies and about 100,000 French settlers scattered in forts and remote areas claimed by France in Canada and along the Ohio River. These forts stopped English colonists from moving westward. The French had extended through the Great Lakes and southward to establish New Orleans in 1718 to service their plantation economy. The Indians also occupied the areas being settled by the English and the French. The relationship between the French and the Indians was more brotherly and closer than the relationship between the English and the Indians. The French were more accepting of the Indians. Traders sometimes married Indian women; many Indians were converted to Catholicism. In the early 1750s the expansion of the French into the Ohio River valley brought British colonial claims into conflict.

During 1754 and 1755 the French were victorious against George Washington and General Edward Braddock at Fort Duquesne. The colonial and English troops did not do so well. At this time, the English were not too interested in what was happening in the colonies. There was a lack of unity among the colonies, and France was far more successful in winning the support of the Indians. The French and Indian War, sometimes known as the Seven Years' War, began in 1756 and lasted until 1763. The colonists were forced to enlist for military duty, and the British troops took whatever supplies they needed from the colonists. They also forced the colonists to shelter British troops without payment.

When William Pitt became the Prime Minister in 1757, he envisioned the colonial conflicts as a step in building a vast British empire. He changed the course of the war by sending more troops and younger, more efficient military leaders, better food, and more weapons and supplies. When the Iroquois who stayed out of the war saw this, they joined the British to fight the French. Prime Minister Pitt borrowed heavily to finance the war. He also paid Prussia to fight in Europe, releasing English troops to fight in the American colonies. Lastly, he reimbursed the colonies for raising troops in North America. In July 1758 the British won their first great victory at Fort Louisbourg, located at the mouth of the St. Lawrence River. Soon after, they took Fort Frontenac. In 1759 General James Wolfe won a spectacular victory in Quebec although the French commander and he were both fatally wounded. When Montreal fell in September 1760, the French lost their last foothold in Canada.

At the peace conference in 1763, the English received Canada and all other French lands east of the Mississippi River from France and Florida from Spain. Spain had joined the French forces against the English. France gave New Orleans and their lands west of the Mississippi River to Spain. The treaty strengthened the American colonies significantly by removing their European rivals and opening the Mississippi Valley to westward expansion. It also expanded the territorial claims of England. The war had been extremely costly. The English government felt that since the colonies had benefited from the war, they should help to defray the expenses. The colonists opposed this. The British felt they should exercise more control and authority over the colonists, who were defying orders and not behaving as "colonies" with a mother country. The colonists resented any intrusions of the English government into their affairs.

The British did not want the colonists to establish new settlements on the frontier because they knew it would create conflicts with the Indians. Therefore, they issued the proclamation of 1763, reserving all the lands west of the Appalachian Mountains for the Indians. This, of course, meant that colonists could not extend the frontier westward. The colonists were very angry.

This was the first time that the colonies had to unite as they fought the French and the Indians. The colonies had to cooperate with the English and among themselves to protect their homes and to bring the war to a successful conclusion. Now, the colonists knew it was possible to create colonial militias, a people's army, to defend themselves against the Indians and even against their mother country, if necessary.

Tensions were developing between England the the colonists. England would not permit the colonists to be represented in Parliament. The colonists did not want to pay taxes to England if they had no voice in the government. Each conflict between the colonists and England increased tensions, eventually leading to the American Revolution.

THE ACADIANS

During one of the earlier wars with France, Great Britain had gained control of Acadia, known today as Nova Scotia, in the Treaty of 1713. The French peasants, living in Acadia, were devout Catholics and hardworking farmers. They tended to be self-sufficient and were not interested in developing commerce and trade with others. According to the Treaty, these original French settlers could become British citizens if they took the oath of allegiance to the British crown. They were permitted to practice their religion; they did not have to learn the English language, be taxed, nor serve in the military. Nevertheless, they still refused to take the oath. The 12,000 Acadians were stubborn and probably still felt a sense of loyalty to their French homeland.

Governor Charles Lawrence of Nova Scotia decided, without consulting people in higher authority, that the Acadians were a threat to the English forces and should be removed from their homes and scattered throughout the colonies. He forcefully and cruelly rounded up about 6,000 of them; others escaped to Canada. He burned their homes and shipped the peasant families to the colonies where the colonists had not been informed that they were to expect "guests." Some of the colonies accepted them, but others refused to allow them to land. Some escaped to islands held by the French in the West Indies. Many of them were able to flee to Louisiana. The ancestors of these people are known today as the "Cajuns." Later some of them returned to Nova Scotia and became British citizens.

Henry Wadsworth Longfellow, in his poem entitled "Evangeline," tells the tragic story about the uprooted Acadians.

1. Why do you think Governor Charles Lawrence thought the Acadians were a threat to the British military forces?

   _____

   _____

   _____

2. Do you think that his plan to remove the Acadians from Nova Scotia was a good one? Why or why not?

   _____

   _____

   _____

3. Tell one way that the Acadians (Cajuns) have influenced American life and culture.

   _____

   _____

   _____

THE FRENCH AND INDIAN WAR

Tell something about how the person, event, or place played a role in the French and Indian War.

1. George Washington _____

2. Edward Braddock _____

3. Fort Duquesne _____

4. Fort Ticonderoga _____

5. William Pitt _____

6. Iroquois Indians _____

7. Colonial militia _____

8. Acadians _____

9. James Wolfe _____

10. Marquis de Montcalm _____

11. Peace of Paris, 1763 _____

12. Proclamation of 1763 _____

SUGGESTED TEACHING ACTIVITIES

1. Topics for further study:
   a. George Washington
   b. Fort Duquesne
   c. Edward Braddock
   d. William Shirley
   e. Acadians
   f. Pontiac
   g. colonial militia
   h. wilderness warfare
   i. British soldiers
   j. Marquis de Montcalm
   k. James Wolfe
   l. William Pitt
   m. Cajuns

2. Map Study: On two outline maps of North America, have students show which European nations had claims to land in North America before and after the Treaty of Paris in 1763. Questions for discussion: Did the Spanish claims increase or decrease? Why? What happened to the French claims after the Treaty of Paris in 1763? Did the English claims increase or decrease? Why?

3. Have students prepare a list of place names which are of French origin.
   Some examples: Eau Claire, Wisconsin   "clear water"
                      Detroit, Michigan   "strait"
   In what part of North America were most of the place names found? Why?

4. Prepare a time line including the following events:
   1. King William's War
   2. Queen Anne's War
   3. King George's War
   4. French and Indian War
   5. British defeat at Fort Duquesne
   6. William Pitt becomes Prime Minister
   7. The Battle of Quebec
   8. Peace of Paris

5. Read selected parts from Henry Wadsworth Longfellow's "Evangeline" to the students. Before reading from the poem, inform students that it is the story about the removal of the Acadians from their homes and the story about two young lovers, Evangeline and Gabriel. On their wedding day, Gabriel was seized and shipped to the colonies. Evangeline spent her lifetime searching for him. She found him as he was dying in the almshouse.
   "Side by side, in their nameless graves, the lovers are sleeping.
   Under the humble walls of the little Catholic churchyard,
   In the heart of the city, they lie, unknown and unnoticed."

Suggestions for Supplementary Reading:

Chidsey, Donald Barr. *The French and Indian War: An Informal History.* New York: Crown Publishers, Inc., 1969.

Russell, Francis. *The French and Indian Wars.* New York: American Heritage Publishing Company, 1962.

CHALLENGING BRITISH AUTHORITY

The British and American colonists celebrated their victories against the French. However, the friendly relations and harmony were short-lived. The British government, the mother country, decided that the colonists had to pay their share of the war debt. As colonists, they had to obey the rules passed by the English Parliament and work for the good of the mother country.

The colonists were angered by the attempt of the British to curtail westward expansion. The Navigation Acts were regarded as outdated and unfair although they were not strictly enforced and infringements were often ignored. Most importantly, they resented laws passed for them by Parliament. They regarded their colonial assemblies as the "Parliament" and the king of England as the authority who had granted their charters. Other reasons for restlessness between the colonies and England were the demeaning treatment of the colonial militia during the French and Indian War, the increasing enforcement of the Navigation Acts, and the effort to establish the Anglican Church in America.

Prime Minister George Grenville felt strongly that the colonies should contribute more monies for the management of the Empire. Parliament passed the Sugar Act in 1764 to eliminate the illegal sugar trade and to raise the duty on sugar and lower the duty on molasses. This act was to be strictly enforced. Commanders of British frigates in American waters would act as customs officers, searching the American ships if necessary. Violators would be tried in courts operated by the British navy. Too, the Prime Minister intended that the colonists pay for a small standing army in America by raising money through the passage of the Stamp Act in 1765. This required that all wills, deeds, and other official and public documents needed to be written on stamped paper or provided with stamps sold by the British government. Patrick Henry, a young lawyer, immediately opposed the Stamp Act and in a speech declared that it was unfair and unjust and would destroy American liberty. It was suggested that a general meeting of committees from all the colonies confer to protest the Stamp Act.

The Stamp Act Congress met and published a "declaration of rights and grievances." In this statement they emphasized that only the colonial assemblies had the right to levy taxes. Copies of this statement were sent to the king and Parliament. The colonists believed it was right for Parliament to regulate foreign trade. However, they were not represented in Parliament; therefore, their colonial assemblies stood in place of Parliament and that was the only body for free English men to use in granting money to the king. The Stamp Act was repealed in 1766. The colonists were overjoyed, but they still had a major grievance regarding the Mutiny or Quartering Act of 1765 which required that the colonists provide quarters and supplies for the British troops.

In 1767 Charles Townshend, minister of finance, introduced new measures which established a board of customs commissioners in America and levied duties on various goods imported to the colonies from England such as lead, paint, glass, paper, and tea. Protests against the Townshend Duties were immediate. The colonists again stated that the British Parliament cannot levy taxes on the colonies to raise revenue and boycotted English goods. The British even sent troops to Boston from Halifax which angered the colonists. When the soldiers were ridiculed by a mob of colonists, they fired into the crowd, killing five citizens and wounding several others. One of the citizens was Crispus Attucks, a mulatto sailor. Samuel Adams called a town meeting in Faneuil Hall and demanded that Governor Hutchinson immediately remove the troops who were responsible for the "Boston Massacre." The British troops were removed.

Because of the petitions from the colonies and the boycott of English goods, the Townshend Duties were repealed. On the day of the Boston Massacre all the duties except the tax on tea were removed. The colonists still refused to buy the tea in American ports. In Boston, the governor was petitioned to send the tea back. He did not do so. On December 16, 1773, a committee of prominent citizens disguised as American Indians boarded the ships, broke the crates with their tomahawks, and threw the tea into the Boston harbor.

The "Boston Tea Party" angered King George. He felt that Boston was the center of protest activities. Therefore, he got parliament to pass the "Intolerable Acts" to punish the state of Massachusetts. The port of Boston was to be closed until the colonists paid for the destroyed tea. Town meetings were forbidden without permission of the governor. Public buildings were to house the British troops. The king's officials, if indicted for capital crimes, were to be returned to England for trial. Expressions of sympathy for Massachusetts were demonstrated by colonists in other colonies. They were irate and restless. When the Virginia Burgesses were dismissed by the royal governor for showing sympathy, they met at the local Raleigh tavern and proposed the first meeting of the Continental Congress, representing committees from all the colonies on September 5, 1774. At that meeting, they discussed the state of the colonies and deliberated on courses of action to take. They also decided to schedule the Second Continental Congress on April 18, 1775.

Before that meeting took place, Governor Thomas Gage sent troops to seize the military weapons hidden by the colonists in Concord. Paul Revere, being informed of this plan, began his midnight ride to warn John Hancock and Samuel Adams that they were to be arrested and that the British troops were on their way to Concord. When the British troops got to Lexington, they found a company of "minutemen" on the village green led by Captain Parker. The British major ordered them to disperse, but the men stood their ground and the British fired, leaving eight of the minutemen dead or dying. The American Revolution began as the colonial militia forced the British troops to retreat from Concord to Boston.

The colonists firmly believed that they had rights as Englishmen—rights such as a fair trial, freedom of speech and assembly, and the right to vote money to fund government through their own colonial assemblies. These rights, they felt, were guaranteed to them by their charters.

PEOPLE AND EVENTS

Many people were involved in the events which eventually led to the American Revolution. They were willing to act upon their beliefs and to take risks to guarantee themselves the freedoms enjoyed by Englishmen.

Match Column I with Column II:

Column I	Column II
_____1. Sugar Act	a. Angry merchants, disguised as Indians, threw tea into the Boston harbor.
_____2. George Grenville	b. This act imposed a tax on every printed document in the colonies such as deeds, newspapers, wills, and mortgages.
_____3. Stamp Act	c. This act required the colonists to provide quarters and supplies for the British troops in America.
_____4. Patrick Henry	d. Taxes levied on various goods imported from England such as lead, paint, paper, and tea
_____5. Quartering Act	e. This act taxed sugar and molasses.
_____6. Townshend Duties	f. He was a citizen killed in the Boston Massacre.
_____7. Charles Townshend	g. This act was passed to punish the protesters in Massachusetts.
_____8. Crispus Attucks	h. He opposed the Stamp Act.
_____9. Boston Massacre	i. He served as a strong minister of finance under Lord Chatham (William Pitt).
_____10. King George	j. He was the commander of the garrison in Boston.
_____11. Boston Tea Party	k. He warned the colonial militia that the British troops were approaching.
_____12. Intolerable Acts	l. The British troops killed five citizens and wounded others in Boston.
_____13. Thomas Gage	m. He became king of Great Britain in 1760.
_____14. Paul Revere	n. He was the prime minister of England in 1764.

WHAT DOES IT MEAN?

Find the definitions of the words listed in the first column:

_____1. propaganda

a. to refuse to buy, sell, or use a product or service to force someone or something to change

_____2. boycott

b. a militia ready to engage in battle at a minute's notice

_____3. repeal

c. the overthrow of a government by force and the establishment of a new one

_____4. minutemen

d. a lawmaking body of England, consisting of the House of Lords and the House of Commons

_____5. duty

e. to tell one side of a story or issue to win support for a cause

_____6. militia

f. a person who uses force to oppose a government

_____7. Parliament

g. officially to cancel or to do away with a law or tax

_____8. rebel

h. to impose or to collect a tax

_____9. revolution

i. an army made up of citizens who serve during times of emergency

_____10. levy

j. a tax paid on products brought into a country

Answer the following questions:

1. Which act was repealed by the English Parliament?

_____

2. When did the colonists boycott English products? What happened as a consequence of the boycott?

_____

_____

_____

3. Do we have anything comparable to the English Parliament in our country? Explain.

_____

_____

_____

SUGGESTED TEACHING ACTIVITIES

1. Topics for further study:
   a. George Grenville
   b. Pontiac
   c. George III
   d. Benjamin Franklin
   e. Boston Tea Party
   f. Quartering Act
   g. tar and feathering
   h. Boston Massacre
   i. Stamp Act
   j. Samuel Adams
   k. militia
   l. "The Parson's Cause"
   m. First Continental Congress
   n. Lexington/Concord Battles
   o. Crispus Attucks
   p. James Otis
   q. Patrick Henry
   r. minutemen
   s. John Hancock
   t. Paul Revere
   u. political cartoons

2. Assign students to prepare a chart listing the Acts passed by the English Parliament to tax the colonists.

Act	Provisions of Act	Reaction of Colonists to Act	Effectiveness of Act	Date of Passage

3. Have students read and dramatize "Paul Revere's Ride" by Henry Wadsworth Longfellow. This poem tells the story of Paul Revere's midnight ride "on the eighteenth of April, in Seventy-five" in Lexington and Concord.

4. Place students in the role of newspaper reporters for the *Boston Gazette*. They will write two articles about the Boston Massacre; one which is written from the point of view of a patriot colonist and one from the point of view of a colonist who still feels loyal to the English crown.

5. Make a time line which includes the following events:
   1. Peace of Paris
   2. Boston Massacre
   3. Boston Tea Party
   4. Intolerable Acts passed
   5. Quartering Act passed
   6. Sugar Act passed
   7. Grenville becomes Prime Minister
   8. Townshend duties imposed
   9. Tea Act passed
   10. Lexington/Concord clash with British troops
   11. Stamp Act passed
   12. First Continental Congress meets

6. Have students answer the following questions regarding the American Revolution:
   a. When did it happen?
   b. Who was involved?
   c. Where did it happen?
   d. Why did it happen?

7. Have students discuss "if" types of questions such as the following:
   a. If you were a merchant in Boston, would you have volunteered to dump the tea in the Boston harbor? Why or why not?
   b. If you were a colonist in Boston, would you have expressed your displeasure with the Stamp Act? Why or why not?
   c. If British soldiers wanted to stay in your home, would you have welcomed them? Why or why not?

8. Assign students to draw political cartoons illustrating their point of view regarding events leading to the American Revolution.

THE WINNING OF INDEPENDENCE

Before the confrontation of the British and the colonists at Lexington and Concord, Patrick Henry, in a speech in Virginia, said, "I know not what course others may take; but as for me, give me liberty or give me death." King George III acknowledged that the military conflict had begun. On the day that the second Continental Congress was scheduled, Ethan Allen and his Green Mountain Boys took Fort Ticonderoga in the name of the Continental Congress.

The British intended to hold the heights which commanded the town of Boston. After valiantly fighting the British, the American militia was forced to abandon its hold on Bunker Hill and Breed's Hill when they ran out of ammunition. This battle demonstrated American courage and steadfastness in spite of the fact that they were defeated. It was a costly British victory. The colonists proved to themselves and to the British that they could compete on the battlefield. At the meeting of the second Continental Congress, the group assumed the powers of a regular government. The Congress issued paper money, made trade regulations, sent representatives to foreign nations, and advised the colonists to set up governments for themselves. George Washington was appointed commander of the Continental Army and, on July 6, 1775, a formal declaration of war was made against Great Britain.

If the colonists had reservations about cutting their ties with Great Britain, a pamphlet, *Common Sense*, helped to convince many to declare themselves patriots seeking independence. *Common Sense* was written by Thomas Paine and distributed early in 1776. The motion declaring independence from the British Crown was passed on July 2, and on July 4 Thomas Jefferson's Declaration of Independence was adopted. This document gave the 13 colonies powers of nationhood. Loyalty to the king now became an act of treason and those guilty were treated as traitors.

After forcing the British to leave Boston, General Washington tried to defend New York, but General Howe's soldiers drove his militia through the city of New York and finally across the state of New Jersey to a safe position on the western bank of the Delaware River. General Washington, though, was not to be defeated; he recrossed the Delaware River, overwhelmed the British army and forced them back to New York. The British were disappointed that the Patriot cause had not yet collapsed. The British strategy was to control the Hudson River, hoping to shut New England off from the southern colonies. They disregarded, however, the conditions of geography and travel in the colonies; they finally surrendered to General Horatio Gates, commander of the Continental

Army on the Hudson River. The total failure of this military strategy left the British without a plan of war.

The British were able to occupy a few seaports such as New York, Newport, and Philadelphia. Because of the American victory at Saratoga, the French, in 1778, signed a treaty of alliance. Each nation was to continue the war with England until the other was ready to make peace. The French provided the Americans with men, money, and a much needed fleet to compete against Britain's naval power. Spain and Holland also joined the Americans against the British. The British left Philadelphia in the summer of 1778 and then moved the center of the war to the South, hoping to separate the states below the Potomac River from the New England colonies. The British did not have a strategic plan. The turning point in the South was the victory of the Americans at King's Mountain, on the border between North and South Carolina.

One of the most distressing incidents of the war involved the betrayal of Benedict Arnold. He fled and was rewarded with a position in the British army. Lord Cornwallis surrendered at Yorktown after being conquered by General Washington and his militia and Marquis de Lafayette and his French troops. New York was the only city now held by the British. Victorious battles were also waging on the frontier. General George Rogers Clark won control of the Northwestern Territory.

King George III abandoned the struggle after the surrender of General Cornwallis at Yorktown. His new prime minister, Lord Shelburne, sent a diplomatic agent to discuss the terms of peace with the American commissioners—John Jay, Benjamin Franklin, and John Adams. There were complications because the Americans had pledged with France that they would not make a separate peace with England. France, Spain, and Holland had helped the Americans win their independence but their primary goal was not accomplished. They had wanted to destroy the naval supremacy of Great Britain and divide up its colonial empire. Americans did feel a great debt to France. Its aid in men, ships, and money helped the patriots win. The commissioners decided to arrange peace terms with England without France. Benjamin Franklin was able to convince the French ministry to accept the terms of the treaty.

The British acknowledged the independence of the United States and the extension of its boundaries to the Mississippi River. They agreed to withdraw their land and naval forces. Fishing rights off Newfoundland and Nova Scotia were granted to the Americans. Secretly, the British agreed to hold the valuable fur trading posts along the Great Lakes until all debts were paid. The rights and properties of Loyalists were to be restored if they had not borne arms against the United States. The British government, surprisingly, granted Loyalists liberal pensions and land in Canada.

On the eighth anniversary of Paul Revere's ride to Concord, Washington proclaimed the end of hostilities with Great Britain. The peace treaty was signed on September 3, 1783, and on November 25 the last British soldiers sailed out of New York harbor. Now, the colonies had the responsibility of developing a structure for a new nation based on a special mission of liberty and justice for all citizens.

STRENGTHS AND WEAKNESSES OF MILITARY FORCES IN THE AMERICAN REVOLUTION

Complete the following chart:

	UNITED STATES	GREAT BRITAIN
Strengths	1. battleground familiar	1. well-trained troops
Weaknesses	1. poorly trained soldiers	1. battleground thousands of miles from Great Britain

1. According to your chart, who should have won the Revolutionary War? Why?

_____

_____

2. Why do you think the Revolutionary War was won by the colonists?

_____

_____

MAJOR INFLUENCES ON AMERICAN THINKING

Read Thomas Paine's pamphlet, *Common Sense*, and Thomas Jefferson's Declaration of Independence.

List two ideas from "Common Sense" and tell how they influenced the thinking of the colonists. Also, comment on how the ideas are a part of our lives today.

_____

_____

_____

_____

_____

List three ideas from the "Declaration of Independence" and tell how they influenced the thinking of the colonists. Also, comment on how the ideas are a part of our lives today.

_____

_____

_____

_____

_____

SUGGESTED TEACHING ACTIVITIES

1. Topics for further study:
   a. role of women
   b. Continental Army
   c. Charles Cornwallis
   d. John Adams
   e. Benjamin Franklin
   f. George Washington
   g. Thomas Paine
   h. Sons of Liberty
   i. Molly Pitcher
   j. John Jay
   k. John Burgoyne
   l. Loyalists
   m. John Paul Jones
   n. Robert Howe
   o. Thomas Jefferson
   p. Liberty Bell
   q. Battle at Saratoga
   r. Valley Forge
   s. Battle at Yorktown
   t. George Rogers Clark
   u. Marquis de Lafayette
   v. Friedrich von Steuben
   w. Benedict Arnold
   x. Abigail Adams

2. Assign students to imagine that their father is serving in General George Washington's Continental Army at Valley Forge. Write a letter to a friend telling how your life and your family's lives on the farm have changed.

3. Assign students to study the American and British flags used during the Revolutionary War. Have them make replicas of the flags and display them in the classroom. Class Discussion: Why do nations have flags? How similar are the American and British flags? How have the flags changed and why?

4. Have student volunteers study a particular Revolutionary War battle. Where did it take place? Why? Who were the important leaders? How important was the battle in determining the victory of the Americans? The strategy used in the battle could be shown on a map.

5. Some students may be interested in volunteering to study and to make special reports or displays of the weapons, ships, military uniforms, assistance for the wounded and dying, and/or communication systems that were used during the Revolutionary War.

6. Have students prepare a list of the names of places (cities, streets) in their communities which have been named after Revolutionary heroes or battles.

Suggestions for Supplementary Reading:

Avi. *The Fighting Ground.* New York: Harper & Row, Publishers, 1984.

Collier, James Lincoln, and Christopher Collier. *My Brother Sam Is Dead.* New York: Scholastic Inc., 1974.

Fast, Howard. *April Morning.* New York: Bantam Books, 1961.

Fleming, Thomas, ed. *Benjamin Franklin: A Biography in His Own Words.* New York: Harper & Row, Publishers, Inc., 1972.

Forbes, Esther. *Johnny Tremain.* Boston: Houghton Mifflin Company, 1943.

O'Dell, Scott. *Sarah Bishop.* New York: Scholastic Inc., 1980.

BEGINNINGS OF A NEW NATION

The military conflict with Great Britain was over. The English colonies were now independent, and the political conflict within America was to begin. The two most important tasks confronted by the colonies were to devise a form of government to ensure stability and security and to settle, develop, and organize its newly acquired western territory.

Between the issuance of the Declaration of Independence and the inauguration of George Washington as the first president of the United States, the nation was governed by a Congress. The Congress included two to seven delegates from each state. They made important decisions because of the state of emergency caused by the Revolutionary War. After the war, a regular national government had to be developed and established.

Before war had been declared against the British, Benjamin Franklin had submitted a draft of the "Articles of Confederation and Perpetual Union" which were largely ignored in 1775. Two years later, a committee prepared the Articles of Confederation which were approved by Congress. It was not until 1781 that all of the states had agreed to accept them. It became the law of the land. Not until the states surrendered their western land claims to the United States did Maryland agree to approve the Articles. As a result of this action the United States acquired thousands of acres of land which could be applied to the payment of the Revolutionary War debt and from which new states could be formed.

The Articles of Confederation were unable to create a strong national government to carry out the powers granted to it. The nations of the world regarded the United States with little respect. The states, protecting their independence and individuality, indulged in petty grievances and confrontations with one another. In Massachusetts, farmers were unable to pay their debts and taxes. Under the leadership of Daniel Shays, a former army officer, the farmers tried to capture the federal arsenal and harassed the merchants and others in the state government. They were easily subdued. Shays and other instigators of the rebellion fled to other states. This rebellion demonstrated the need to revise or replace the Articles for a stronger Confederation. Congress was weak and powerless; very few states even bothered to send their seven representatives to the meetings. There was no United States government.

In spite of its weakness, Congress did pass a remarkable piece of legislation, the Northwest Ordinance of 1787. This ordinance organized the Northwest Territory which was to be governed by a governor and three judges until the population was large enough for representative government. The citizens were guaranteed political and religious freedom, and the practice of slavery was prohibited. A system of free public education was provided. Eventually from three to five new states could be formed out of this territory.

Changes in the structure of government were necessary. Finally, Congress officially proposed a convention of delegates from all the states to revise the Articles of Confederation. This occurred because of a conflict between Maryland and Virginia over the control of the Potomac River. When representatives of these two states met with George Washington to settle the matter, they realized that other states were also involved. A meeting was scheduled at Annapolis, Maryland to consider the commercial interests of the United States. When the delegates met in 1786, they discussed the commercial issues, and they wanted to discuss other important matters. Another meeting was scheduled for a revision of the Articles of Confederation at Independence Hall in Philadelphia in May 1787. Only Rhode Island refused to send delegates.

At the Convention, various plans such as the Virginia Plan and the New Jersey Plan were presented and debated. The new government had to satisfy those who favored strong states and those who favored a strong central government by distributing power between the central and state governments. James Madison developed a compromise plan that separated the responsibilities of the legislative, executive, and judicial branches of government. Each branch would operate independently but have a check on the other.

Several other compromises on important issues were finally accepted. The states were to preserve their equality of representation in the Senate. In the House of Representatives, the members were to be elected by the people of the states; the number of representatives from each state depended upon its population. Three-fifths of the slaves were to be counted in making up the apportionment for Congress. Congress was prohibited from interfering with the slave trade for 20 years. Tariff laws were to be passed by a simple majority vote and no duties were to be levied on exports. A four-year term was approved for the presidency. These were a few of the compromises.

After 11 states had ratified the new Constitution, it became the supreme law for those states. North Carolina did not ratify it until Washington had been president for over six months. Rhode Island ratified the Constitution when it was threatened to be treated as a foreign nation in its commerce with other states. Without violence or bloodshed, Americans adopted the "Constitution of the United States of the people, by the people, and for the people." The new nation had moved from anarchy, no government, to a country of strength and power. Peaceful debate and compromise among reasonable people changed the governmental structure into a strong and stable symbol of liberty under law.

THE CONSTITUTION—DOCUMENT OF FREEDOM

The Preamble: The Purpose of the Constitution

We, the people of the United States, in order to form a more perfect Union, establish justice, insure domestic tranquillity, provide for the common defense, promote the general welfare, and secure the blessings of liberty to ourselves and our posterity, do ordain and establish this Constitution for the United States of America.

Answer the following questions regarding the Constitution:

1. What are the qualifications of a person who wants to be a member of the House of Representatives? A member of the Senate?

   _____

   _____

2. What are at least three important powers of Congress?

   _____

   _____

   _____

3. What are the qualifications of a person who wants to be president of the United States? Do you think a woman or a black might fulfill these qualifications? Do you think a woman or a black might become president of the United States within the next 25 years? Explain.

   _____

   _____

   _____

   _____

4. What are the powers of the president? Do you think that the president has too many responsibilities for one person? Explain.

   _____

   _____

5. How does one become a justice of the Supreme Court?

   _____

6. What are the responsibilities of the Supreme Court?

   _____

7. What is meant by the term *checks and balances*?

   _____

8. Why is Article V: "Amending the Constitution" important in a democracy?

   _____

THE BILL OF RIGHTS

James Madison presented a set of amendments to protect individual rights in a democracy. These 10 amendments to the Constitution are known as the Bill of Rights, and they went into effect in 1791. Since that time many more amendments have been added.

For each of the amendments, write one or two sentences telling how it safeguards individual rights and how it affects your daily life.

Amendment 1:   Freedom of Religion, Speech, Press, Assembly, and Petition _____

_____

Amendment 2:   Right to Bear Arms_____

_____

Amendment 3:   Quartering of Soldiers _____

_____

Amendment 4:   Search and Seizure _____

_____

Amendment 5:   Rights of Accused Persons _____

_____

Amendment 6:   Right to Speedy and Public Trial _____

_____

Amendment 7:   Trial by Jury in Civil Cases _____

_____

Amendment 8:   Limits of Fines and Punishments _____

_____

Amendment 9:   Rights of the People _____

_____

Amendment 10:   Powers of the States and People _____

_____

A. Which two amendments do you think are the most important? Why?

_____

_____

B. Which two amendments do you think are no longer as important as they were during the late 1700s and early 1800s? Explain.

_____

_____

1. Topics for further study:
   a. House of Representatives
   b. Senate
   c. James Madison
   d. Alexander Hamilton
   e. Northwest Ordinance of 1787
   f. Ratification of Constitution
   g. Shays's Rebellion
   h. Virginia Plan
   i. New Jersey Plan
   j. Federalism
   k. Separation of Powers
   l. *The Federalist Papers*

2. Have students prepare a time line to include the following events:
   1. Shays's Rebellion
   2. Constitutional Convention in Philadelphia
   3. Ratification of Constitution by Rhode Island
   4. Ratification of Constitution by Delaware
   5. Publication of *The Federalist Papers*
   6. Northwest Ordinance
   7. Approval of Articles of Confederation
   8. Approval of Bill of Rights

3. Have students prepare a chart with two columns and list the powers granted to each government.

Powers of the Confederation Government	Powers of the Constitutional Government

4. Read to the class excerpts from Benjamin Franklin's *The Autobiography*. Questions for Class Discussion: What role did Benjamin Franklin play at the Constitutional Convention? How important were his contributions in developing the structure of our government? How was he able to bring about harmony and compromise among the delegates? To make money Franklin published *Poor Richard's Almanack* which was a financial success. Every house needed a calendar. Franklin also included weather forecasts, jokes, maxims, and other features. Students may discuss or write about some of the "sayings of Poor Richard" such as the following ones.

   Three may keep a secret if two of them are dead.
   Fish and visitors smell in three days.
   He that composes himself is wiser than he that composes books.
   Tis hard for an empty bag to stand upright.
   A small leak will sink a great ship.

5. Have students prepare speeches to present before the Constitutional Convention in Philadelphia supporting approval or disapproval of the New Jersey Plan, the Virginia Plan, or a compromise. These presentations may be made before the class and discussed.

LAUNCHING THE NEW GOVERNMENT

The nation who voted George Washington unanimously to the presidency in 1789 was very different from the United States of today. The population at that time was 3,292,214, which is considerably less than the 1990 population of 7,322,564 for New York City alone. About 90 percent of the people were farmers. If they were not farmers, they were probably involved in fishing and shipping. England had discouraged the development of industries in the colonies. During the 1790s Americans were temporarily satisfied with selling agricultural products for England's manufactured goods. Land was abundant and the government encouraged the sale and settlement of lands west of the Alleghenies.

Poor and scarce roads and the lack of comfortable transportation vehicles made traveling to New York City difficult. It was not until the inauguration of President Washington on April 30, 1789, that Congress was organized and the electoral votes counted. President Washington appointed Thomas Jefferson as his secretary of state and Alexander Hamilton as his secretary of the treasury. Hamilton and Jefferson held different views about the role of government. They often disagreed and exhibited their anger at cabinet meetings. Both men begged Washington to choose between them and let the other resign. He did not and asked them to remain during the first term of his presidency, which they did.

Congress was confronted with enormous tasks such as creating the departments of Congress, courts, and post offices; adopting the Bill of Rights; dealing with Indian conflicts; taking the census; setting the salaries of federal employees; and voting appropriations to manage the new government.

Hamilton was able to meet the challenge of establishing the credit of the United States and providing an adequate income to manage the government. He insisted in paying the national debt in full and assuming the Revolutionary War debts of the various states. This action strengthened the political power of the United States. To pay the national and state debts, Hamilton proposed an excise tax on distilled liquors and a tariff, less than 10 percent, on imported goods to meet the nation's monetary needs. This tariff encouraged American manufacturers by protecting them from foreign competition and made way for the eventual development of industries. Another proposal was to create a National Bank, chartered by Congress, which would handle governmental financial transactions. There was much opposition to Hamilton's proposals.

The controversies about the role of government led to the development of political parties. One party, the Federalists, emerged under Hamilton's leadership which advocated a strong central government and a loose interpretation of the Constitution. They believed that only a selected group of successful, able, and "well-born" individuals could govern the nation best. Jefferson's Democratic-Republican Party favored agriculture over manufacturing and had confidence in the ordinary citizen. This party believed in a strict interpretation of the Constitution and opposed popular taxation. "Government should be for the people and by the people" was strongly endorsed by Jefferson. Washington, leaning toward the Federalists, was unanimously reelected for a second term in 1792 and Hamilton's financial policies were passed. Jefferson and Edmund Randolph resigned from the cabinet.

In 1793 the French were at war in Europe. During the Revolutionary War, the French king, now overthrown and guillotined, had sent money, men, and ships to aid the colonists against the English. The 1778 Treaty of Alliance with France pledged assistance to France to defend her possessions and to allow the use of American ports. The treaty had been signed by King Louis XVI, not with the faction that overthrew him. Washington, therefore, issued the proclamation of neutrality in 1793 which stated that the United States would remain neutral in European hostilities. "Citizen" Edmond Genet, a French minister, came to the United States and openly defied the proclamation. He conducted himself in a manner unbecoming of a foreign official; he was sent back to France.

Washington believed it was important to maintain peace with Great Britain and Spain. The British still held fortified posts on the Great Lakes, and they were not willing to give up the valuable fur trade since American merchants still owed large debts to England. American ships were stopped on the seas by the British to search for deserters from the British Navy. They impressed American citizens into British service. John Jay was sent to Great Britain to negotiate a new treaty which was ratified by the Senate in spite of the opposition to it. The English agreed to vacate the posts by June 1796, and to submit to arbitration disputed boundaries, damages to American shipping, and the debts due to British merchants. When Jay went to England, Thomas Pinckney went to Spain and negotiated a treaty in which Spain recognized the thirty-first parallel as the boundary between Florida and the United States. The treaty also granted Americans free navigation of the Mississippi with the "right of deposit" at New Orleans; American ships would not have to pay any duty. When a few frontier farmers organized the "Whiskey Rebellion," defying the taxes on whiskey distilleries, Washington sent out the army which quickly crushed the rebellion.

In 1796 John Adams became the second president of the United States, and he found himself immediately entangled in a conflict with the French who tried to secure a loan and a bribe from the Americans. With British cooperation, Adams signed a treaty with Napoleon Bonaparte of France which canceled the treaty of 1789 and established new commercial arrangements. In 1789 the naturalization law was passed which increased the term of residency to 14 years for a foreigner to become a citizen. John Adams signed the Alien Act which gave the president power to deport foreigners and the Sedition Act which provided imprisonment or fines for anyone speaking, writing, or printing anything critical of the government.

The Federalist period was important in strengthening the unity of the nation, in setting up a stable governmental structure, and in gaining respect among other nations. Also, it was a time of growth and prosperity in the economy.

WHICH EVENT HAPPENED FIRST?

Place the letter of the event that happened first in the blank at the left.

_____1. a. George Washington, a Federalist, is reelected unanimously for a second term as president of the United States.
        b. King Louis XVI is overthrown and executed by French citizens.

_____2. a. The French Revolution begins.
        b. John Adams is elected the second president of the United States.

_____3. a. The Jay Treaty requires the removal of British trading posts, fortifications, and troops from the Great Lakes area.
        b. The Treaty of Paris with Great Britain recognizes the independence of the 13 colonies.

_____4. a. Thomas Jefferson resigns as secretary of state from President George Washington's cabinet.
        b. The "Whiskey Rebellion," led by farmers objecting to the tax on whiskey they made, fails when President Washington sends the federal troops to Pennsylvania.

_____5. a. George Washington issues his "Farewell Address."
        b. The Citizen Genet Affair challenges President Washington's proclamation of neutrality.

_____6. a. The Sedition Act, which imposes fines or prison terms for individuals writing, speaking, or printing anything critical of the government, is signed by President John Adams.
        b. Thomas Jefferson becomes the third president of the nation.

_____7 a. The new government assembles in New York City, the temporary capital, for the first time.
        b. The Constitution of the United States is adopted.

_____8. a. The National Bank of the United States, proposed by Alexander Hamilton, is chartered by Congress.
        b. Thomas Paine publishes the pamphlet, *Common Sense*.

_____9. a. The Pinckney Treaty with Spain provides Americans with access to the Mississippi River for transportation and the use of New Orleans as a seaport.
        b. The Constitutional Convention meets in Philadelphia.

_____10. a. The Bill of Rights is adopted by Congress.
        b. The Alien Act is signed by President John Adams.

WHAT DOES IT MEAN?

Match the definitions in Column II with the terms they define in Column I.

COLUMN I

_____1. Constitution

_____2. impressment

_____3. excise tax

_____4. tariff

_____5. loose construction

_____6. Federalists

_____7. Democratic-Republicans

_____8. Sedition Act

_____9. Alien Act

_____10. Naturalization Act

_____11. proclamation of neutrality

_____12. "right of deposit"

_____13. cabinet

_____14. strict construction

COLUMN II

a. a tax on certain goods produced, sold, or used within a country

b. an interpretation of the Constitution holding that the federal government has broad powers

c. gave the president power to deport aliens judged to be dangerous to the peace and safety of the United States

d. the act of forcing individuals into public service against their will

e. an interpretation of the Constitution holding that the powers of the federal government are strictly defined

f. a tax or duty on imported goods and products

g. heads of executive departments who advise the president

h. the right to unload cargoes from ships

i. A person may be fined or imprisoned for writing, speaking, or printing false or malicious statements against the government.

j. They advocated government "for the people and by the people."

k. increased from 5 to 14 years, the term of residence in the United States necessary to make a foreigner a citizen

l. They advocated a strong central government.

m. a policy of the United States to keep detached from the complicated conflicts in Europe

n. a document which includes the basic principles and laws describing the structure of government

SUGGESTED TEACHING ACTIVITIES

1. Topics for further study:
   - a. Thomas Jefferson
   - b. Alexander Hamilton
   - c. National Bank
   - d. Federalists
   - e. Democratic-Republicans
   - f. Martha Washington
   - g. Abigail Adams
   - h. "Citizen" Edmond Genet
   - i. Napoleon Bonaparte
   - j. Tallyrand
   - k. John Marshall
   - l. midnight judges
   - m. John Jay
   - n. Whiskey Rebellion
   - o. C. C. Pinckney
   - p. Thomas Pinckney
   - q. Jay Treaty
   - r. Pinckney Treaty
   - s. Virginia and Kentucky Resolutions
   - t. Washington's Farewell Address
   - u. French Revolution
   - v. "XYZ Affair"

2. Ask students to bring in political cartoons from their home newspapers. Discuss the purpose of political cartoons, analyzing the issues depicted in the cartoons. Have students draw political cartoons showing the different reactions to the Alien and Sedition Acts. Questions for discussion:
   1. Why were some people opposed to the acts?
   2. Why were some citizens supporting these acts?
   3. Was the opposition along party lines? Why or why not?
   4. How effective were the Virginia and Kentucky Resolutions?
   5. Do you think that these acts were constitutional? Why or why not?

3. Class Discussion: What kind of a first lady was Martha Washington? Abigail Adams? How has the role of the first lady changed? What is Hillary R. Clinton's perception of the first lady's role? Explain. What do you think should be the first lady's role?

4. Assign students to study aspects of life during the Federalist Era. Divide the class into four groups. Each group will make an intensive study about the listed topics and report their findings to the class. The topics are inventions and factories, roads and transportation facilities, post office services and money, and clothing for men, women, and children.

5. Assign students to write a short composition telling which political party they would support and why if they were citizens during the administrations of George Washington and John Adams.

Suggestions for Supplementary Reading:

Boller, Jr., Paul F. *Presidential Wives: An Anecdotal History.* New York: Oxford University Press, 1988.

Desmond, Alice Curtis. *Martha Washington: Our First Lady.* New York: Dodd, Mead & Company, 1957.

Faber, Doris. *John Jay.* New York: G. P. Putnam's Sons, 1966.

Meltzer, Milton. *George Washington and the Birth of Our Nation.* New York: Franklin Watts, 1986.

---.*Thomas Jefferson: The Revolutionary Aristocrat.* New York: Franklin Watts, 1991.

Wise, William. *Alexander Hamilton.* New York: G. P. Putnam's Sons, 1963.

ERA OF JEFFERSONIAN POLICIES

The Republicans gained control of the federal government in 1801. They favored independent farmers and rural communities, education for male citizens, cultural independence from Europe, and a federal government with limited power. The major task of federal government was only to manage foreign affairs. This was not to be the way they planned. Commerce was expanding, and the economy was becoming diverse and complex. The beginnings of the industrial revolution were in progress in England. Power-driven machines were replacing hand-operated tools. Samuel Slater built a spinning mill in Rhode Island, the first modern factory in this country, in 1790. Other factories were being built. Inventions created by Robert Fulton, Eli Whitney, and others were changing American life. Cities were growing and the population and the land area of the United States were increasing. The social and economic aspects of American life were changing. Many times, the Republicans advocated one thing and did another; American political life was also changing.

Thomas Jefferson assumed the presidency in the newly designed capital, Washington, D.C. The Twelfth Amendment was added to the Constitution in 1804 eliminating a tie between the president and vice-president of the same party. Jefferson introduced a strict economy in governmental expenditures, cutting taxes, and reducing the size of the army and navy. Nevertheless, he stretched the Constitution and spent more money than any Federalist had before him.

Napoleon Bonaparte, emperor of France, planned to establish a colonial empire in the New World. He signed a secret treaty with Spain in 1800 which gave him the land west of the Mississippi River to the Rocky Mountains, stretching south from the Canadian border to the Gulf of Mexico. When Jefferson learned about this treaty, he was disturbed and concerned about American commerce and the control of New Orleans. In 1802 Napoleon withdrew the right of Americans to use the port of New Orleans to transport their products as guaranteed in the Treaty of 1795. Jefferson sent James Monroe to Paris to assist Robert R. Livingston, the minister in Paris, in purchasing New Orleans and West Florida. In the meantime, Napoleon had abandoned his plans for a colonial empire and had decided to continue his struggle for world leadership in Europe. After negotiating with Talleyrand, the French foreign minister, Monroe and Livingston, without consulting President Jefferson, paid $15,000,000 for the Louisiana Purchase on April 30, 1803. This Purchase was one of the most significant events in U.S. history. It doubled the area of the United States and expanded its power over a rich, fertile area of land. Eventually 14 states were created from this purchase.

Today the area is productive in cattle, timber, wheat, corn, sugar, and cotton, returning Jefferson's investment many times over.

Less than two months after the Louisiana purchase, Jefferson commissioned Captain Meriwether Lewis to direct a scientific exploring party to the lands west of the Mississippi River. Captain Lewis enlisted the aid of William Clark, and they began their expedition in the spring of 1804 with a company of about 50 men. At Fort Bismarck, Sacagawea, a Shoshoni, joined the group and served as interpreter and guide. From St. Louis they followed the Missouri River to its source, crossed the Rockies, and finally followed the Columbia River to the sea. They made important studies of the natural features of the country and the culture of the Indian tribes in their two-and-a-half-year journey. Their remarkable expedition was an important factor in the dispute with England over the Oregon country 40 years later.

There is no clause in the Constitution of the United States that provides the president with the right to purchase foreign territory. Jefferson, a strict constructionist of the Constitution, was somewhat disturbed by his own action in purchasing the land. The country, though, enthusiastically endorsed the purchase. In 1804 Jefferson was reelected. United States' territory had doubled, the debt had been reduced, and the people were united.

Since Aaron Burr was not selected as vice-president for Jefferson's second term, he decided to run for governor of New York. He was defeated because of Alexander Hamilton's efforts. He challenged Hamilton to a duel and mortally wounded him with the first shot on July 11, 1804. No one knew exactly what Burr wanted to do. Some thought he wanted to establish an independent state in the Mississippi Valley; others thought he was planning to seize the city of New Orleans and carve an empire for himself. In 1807 Burr was captured while trying to escape to Spanish Florida and was brought to Richmond for trial. John Marshall, the Chief Justice of the Supreme Court, presided over the trial and found no reason to convict Burr of treason.

Napoleon still wished to dominate the continent. He was successful on land but Britain still controlled the seas. Napoleon was unable to destroy the British fleet; therefore, he decided he would destroy her commerce. He ordered, in 1806, the seizure of any ships that had touched a British port. Great Britain, in turn, prohibited neutral vessels to trade with any countries under Napoleon's control unless such ships had touched at a British port. The English seized the merchant vessels that had not touched British ports, and the French seized those that had. The United States had built up an immense volume of shipping all over the world. It was this prosperous foreign trade that was threatened by France and England. British ships stopped U. S. ships, boarding them and taking off hundreds of sailors, supposedly suspecting deserters from the British Navy.

In June, 1807, the British ship *Leopard* opened fire on the U. S. *Chesapeake* when the commander refused to let his ship be searched for deserters. Three of the *Chesapeake's* men were killed and 18 wounded before the commander surrendered. Americans were outraged. Congress passed the Embargo Act of December 22, 1807, which forbade all ships to leave American harbors for foreign ports. The shipowners accused Jefferson of trying to ruin their shipping business. It was finally repealed in March 2, 1809.

Name_____

THE UNITED STATES IN 1804

On the outline map below, identify the American lands as of 1804:

    a. the states and territories east of the Mississippi River

    b. the Louisiana Purchase

Also, identify the routes taken by the expeditions of Lewis and Clark and Zebulon M. Pike and the lands claimed by Great Britain, Spain, and Russia.

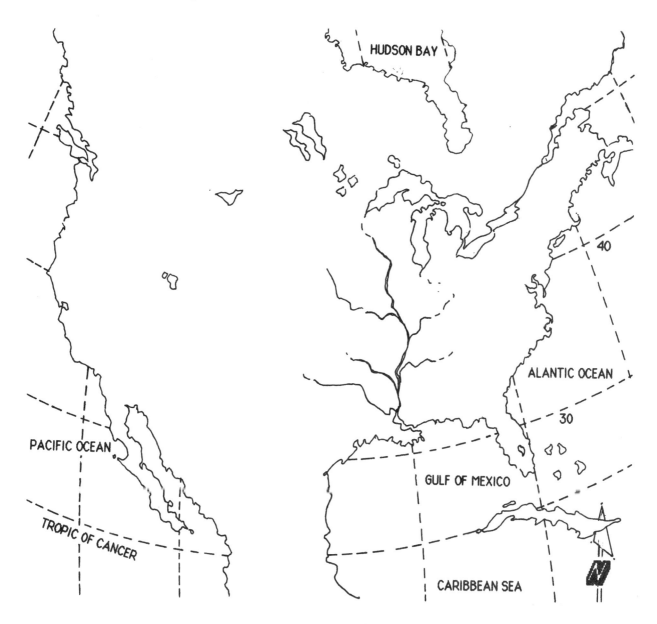

NATIONAL CENSUSES

The Constitution mandates that a national census be taken regularly to determine the number of representatives each state would have in the House of Representatives. This has been accomplished since 1790. Today, the census data are used in many ways in addition to the original use for legislative apportionment.

Study the following table:

YEAR	RESIDENT POPULATION	LAND AREA SQUARE MILES
1790	3,929,214	864,746
1800	5,308,483	864,746
1810	7,239,881	1,681,828
1820	9,638,453	1,749,462
1830	12,866,020	1,749,462
1840	17,069,453	1,749,462

Make a bar graph showing the increase in population and land area.

What are some inferences that can be made from the data?

_____

_____

_____

_____

SUGGESTED TEACHING ACTIVITIES

1. Topics for further study:
   - a. universal education
   - b. Massachusetts law of 1789
   - c. Jedidiah Morse
   - d. Judith Sargent Murray
   - e. Washington Irving
   - f. Mercy Otis Warren
   - g. religious camp meetings
   - h. John Marshall
   - i. Meriwether Lewis
   - j. Samuel Slater
   - k. Oliver Evans
   - l. Eli Whitney
   - m. Pierre L'Enfant
   - n. Barbary Wars
   - o. U.S. Military Academy at West Point
   - p. James Watt
   - q. Monticello
   - r. Sacagawea
   - s. Aaron Burr
   - t. Noah Webster
   - u. William Clark
   - v. turnpikes

2. Assign students to prepare a time line to include the following events:
   1. Election of George Washington
   2. Election of John Adams
   3. Election of Thomas Jefferson
   4. Lewis and Clark Expedition
   5. Zebulon Pike's Expedition
   5. U.S. Military Academy founded at West Point
   7. U.S. capital moves to Washington, D.C.
   8. Sedition Act
   9. The Louisiana Purchase
   10. Invention of cotton gin
   11. Steam engine patented
   12. Approval of Constitution

3. Assign students to review John Marshall's years as Chief Justice of the Supreme Court and the decision of the case, *Marbury v. Madison* (1803). Who was Marbury? Madison? Why was the decision made by Justice Marshall so important? What is meant by "judicial review"? Do you think the authors of the Constitution had this in mind when they created the Supreme Court? How does this power of the Supreme Court reflect the "checks and balances" in the structure of our government?

4. Place students in the role of being members of the Lewis and Clark or Pike Expeditions. Have them keep a journal (at least five entries) of their experiences as they reach their destination and return to report to President Jefferson. Students should note geography, Indians, animals, trees and land.

5. If possible, visit a local museum that has paintings, sculptures, and other arts illustrating the events which occurred during the first decade of the nineteenth century, the Jeffersonian era. Have students list the art (painting or sculpture), artist, year work completed, event being depicted, and their impressions of the work based on their study of history.

Suggestions for Supplemental Reading:

Phelan, Mary Kay. *The Story of the Louisiana Purchase*. Illustrated by Frank Aloise. New York: Thomas Y. Crowell, 1979.

Tallant, Robert. *The Louisiana Purchase*. New York: Random House, 1952.

Tunis, Edwin. *The Young United States: 1783 to 1830*. New York: The World Publishing Company, 1969.

CONFLICTS WITH THE BRITISH AND THE INDIANS

Three days after the repeal of the Embargo Act and the enactment of the Non-Intercourse Act, James Madison, a Republican, assumed the presidency of the United States. The new act opened trade with all nations except Great Britain and France. In 1810, when this act expired, it was replaced by the Macon's Bill No. 2 which reopened trade with any nation, including Great Britain and France. President Madison had demonstrated notable leadership in helping to frame the Constitution. As president, he was unable to make intelligent political decisions. He wanted to continue peace with Great Britain, but he never developed a plan for peace nor did he prepare for war.

The blockade was only one of the grievances against Great Britain. Americans blamed the British for the Indian raids in the Northwest. Tecumseh, an intelligent and courageous Indian leader, had organized a confederation of tribes to resist the westward expansion of Americans over their lands. In November, 1811, General William Henry Harrison, governor of the Northwest, defeated Tecumseh and his followers at Tippecanoe Creek in the Indiana Territory. Harrison reported that the Indians had huge supplies of the best British guns and other weapons. The suspicions of the government that the British had been inciting the Indians was confirmed.

The new Congress convened in early winter of 1811. A group of Congressmen, known as "War Hawks" were determined that the independence and dignity of the United States should be respected by foreign powers. They wanted more land—Canada and lands held by Indians, even Florida. The leader of the "War Hawks" was Henry Clay, a young law student, possessing intelligence and a gift of oratory. As Speaker of the House, he appointed committees. It became evident that those supporting war with Great Britain were in positions of authority. President Madison sent Congress a list of the hostile acts performed by Great Britain. Congress declared war against Great Britain on June 18, 1812. President Madison was unaware that the British had changed their policy. Now, they wanted to avoid war. Their economy was suffering, and the blockade of Europe was repealed in June. New England merchants and shippers opposed the war while the rest of the country strongly supported it.

The United States was not prepared for war. The army had few soldiers, many of them recently recruited, who had been trained under inexperienced commanders. The navy had only 15 ships. Vermont and Connecticut refused to provide soldiers for the army. During the war New Englanders sold beef and other products to the British in Canada. In 1812, General William Hull, in a court martial, was sentenced to death for abandoning his post in Detroit. Hull's action gave the British control of Lake Erie. Later, General Harrison was able to retake Detroit and drive the British across the Detroit River. Conquering Canada was not as easy as predicted by the "War Hawks."

The victory of Oliver Hazard Perry on Lake Erie ended with the famous message, "We have met the enemy and they are ours." The British blockade of American ports was successful; shipping to anywhere was brought to a halt. In August, 1814, a small British force from Chesapeake Bay raided Washington. They burned the White House, the Capitol, and other buildings and caused much damage. The British continued their march to Fort McHenry near Baltimore. The Maryland militia and the zealous defense of Fort McHenry stopped the British. The sight of the American flag waving at Fort McHenry inspired Francis Scott Key to write "The Star-Spangled Banner." The British and the Americans were ready for peace.

When the war between Napoleon and Great Britain ended, the peace treaty was signed at Ghent on December 24, 1814, in the Netherlands, restoring the conditions as they existed before the war. The settlement of boundary disputes was referred to commissioners. Before the news of the peace treaty reached America, Andrew Jackson, a Tennessee Indian fighter, commanded a small army which forcibly drove the British back in the Battle of New Orleans on January 8, 1815. Andrew Jackson emerged as a national hero.

After the peace treaty, the United States ignored Europe and confronted the problems of a growing and developing nation. Before the war, thousands of pioneers had crossed the Alleghenies into the Ohio and Tennessee valleys. The Indians, encouraged by England on the north and by Spain on the south, were a constant threat to settlers. Poor roads made it necessary to find lands near navigable rivers. In the 1810s these difficulties and hindrances to westward expansion were slowly being removed. The victories of General Harrison and General Jackson put an end to the danger from Indians on the frontiers. In 1811 the steamboat made its first appearance on the Ohio River. It was now easier to ship crops from Louisville to New Orleans.

Many families moved westward, buying land cheaply from the government. Immigrants from Europe sought farmlands on the frontier. With the invention of machinery in England for spinning and weaving, demand for cotton increased. The cotton planters moved westward and opened up new plantations. President Madison urged that roads be built to draw the nation together. The bill was defeated. The president believed that an amendment to the Constitution was needed to accomplish this.

Florida, to the Americans, was a refuge for Indians, runaway slaves, and criminals who terrorized the South and prevented development in the states immediate to its north. Americans believed that the Gulf of Mexico was a "natural boundary" on the south. The United States offered to buy the land, but Spain was not willing to sell. In 1818, President Monroe ordered General Andrew Jackson to halt the Indian raids from Florida. General Jackson did more than that, he invaded and conquered Florida. The United States was embarrassed; American troops were removed. Spain, with many problems in Europe, decided to sign a treaty with the United States in 1819 in which she gave up her claims to Florida.

DOLLEY MADISON, FIRST LADY

Before Dolley Madison's husband became president, she performed as a part-time hostess for President Thomas Jefferson, a widower. When James Madison became president, she was already known as an attractive and charming first lady. She was strong-minded, energetic, and intelligent and possessed a remarkable memory for names and faces. At presidential receptions, dinners, and social gatherings, she exhibited kindness and friendliness and was known as an outstanding hostess.

When President Madison was notified that the British had landed in Maryland and were marching toward Washington, he told his wife to leave immediately for Virginia while he inspected the army headquarters in the capital. She insisted, though, on remaining in her home until she was sure he was safe. On August 24, 1814, as she was about to have her lunch, she heard the British guns and cannons. She had no choice but to leave. She rushed out and ordered her carriage and wagon to be brought to the door. She and her friends and servants loaded the wagon with papers, books, notes, and other presidential valuables. She asked a young lieutenant to get the famous Gilbert Stuart portrait of George Washington from the president's house. Now, she was ready to leave Washington to stay with friends in Virginia. Not long after her departure, the untrained militia and government officials also fled from the city into Virginia. The British burned the White House, the Capitol, and other governmental buildings and caused over a million dollars worth of damage on the city. When a thunderstorm broke, the British left Washington.

What does this story tell you about the kind of person Dolley Madison was?

_____

_____

Tell something interesting, in three or four sentences, about each first lady:

1. Martha Washington _____

_____

2. Abigail Adams _____

_____

3. Martha Jefferson _____

_____

4. Dolley Madison_____

_____

5. Elizabeth Monroe _____

_____

PEOPLE, EVENTS, AND TERMS

Write the letter of the correct "match" for each person, event, and term.

_____1. Henry Clay

a. Home designed by Thomas Jefferson

_____2. Francis Scott Key

b. "Hero of New Orleans"

_____3. William Hull

c. Made its appearance on Ohio River in 1811

_____4. William H. Harrison

d. Signed in 1814; it restored the conditions as they existed before the war

_____5. frigates

e. Commander at Detroit who was court-martialed for abandoning his post

_____6. impressment

f. Fought with the British in War of 1812

_____7. Chesapeake Affair

g. Congress prohibited all ships to leave American ports for foreign ports.

_____8. Embargo Act

h. Speaker of the House who advocated war with Great Britain and led the "War Hawks"

_____9. James Madison

i. Wrote "The Star-Spangled Banner"

_____10. Treaty of Ghent

j. To withdraw officially from membership in an alliance or organization

_____11. Andrew Jackson

k. Defeated the Indians at Tippecanoe Creek in Indiana territory

_____12. cede

l. The fourth president of the United States

_____13. secede

m. Three seamen were killed and 18 wounded in this confrontation

_____14. Tecumseh

n. To transfer officially the right of ownership

_____15. steamboat

o. Practice of stopping and boarding American ships and forcing American sailors into British naval service

_____16. Monticello

p. Fast, medium-sized sailing warships

SUGGESTED TEACHING ACTIVITIES

1. Topics for further study:
   - a. Hartford Convention
   - b. "Old Ironsides"
   - c. Panic of 1819
   - d. Dolley Madison
   - e. James Madison
   - f. frigates
   - g. steamboats
   - h. Andrew Jackson
   - i. Cherokee Indians
   - h. Seminole Indians
   - j. Shawnee Indians
   - k. Oliver H. Perry

2. Assign students to identify the person who made each of the following quotes. Also evaluate their appropriateness:
   - a. "Mr. Madison's war."
   - b. "We have met the enemy and they are ours."
   - c. "Whose broad stripes and bright stars, through the perilous fight, O'er the ramparts we watched were so gallantly streaming!"

3. Assign students to make a line graph showing the value of exports (red pencil) and imports (blue pencil) in millions of dollars between 1800 and 1820.

YEAR	VALUE OF EXPORTS	VALUE OF IMPORTS	YEAR	VALUE OF EXPORTS	VALUE OF IMPORTS
1800	71	91	1811	61	53
1801	93	111	1812	39	77
1802	72	76	1813	28	22
1803	56	65	1814	7	13
1804	78	85	1815	53	113
1805	96	121	1816	82	147
1806	102	129	1817	88	99
1807	108	139	1818	93	122
1808	22	57	1819	70	87
1809	52	59	1820	70	74
1810	67	85			

What reasons can you give for the increases and decreases in the value of exports? The value of imports? Does your line graph tell you why shipowners, merchants, and planters were in support of the War of 1812? In opposition to the war? List the inferences which can be made from this graph.

4. Assign students to identify on an outline map all of the states and the territories of the United States as of 1822. How has it changed since President Jefferson made the Louisiana purchase from France?

5. On a time line, have students include the following events:
   - a. James Madison is elected president
   - b. Spain cedes Florida to the United States
   - c. Battle of Tippecanoe
   - d. James Monroe is elected president
   - e. U.S. victory in New Orleans
   - f. Declaration of war with British
   - g. Writing of "The Star-Spangled Banner"
   - h. Treaty of Ghent

Suggestions for Supplementary Reading:

Marrin, Albert. *1812: The War Nobody Won*. New York: Atheneum, 1985.

AMERICAN NATIONALISM AND SECTIONALISM

After the War of 1812, many social, economic, and political changes took place as the nation grew and expanded. Thousands of acres of cotton were planted in the South to meet the needs of an increasing market. In the North new factories were being built. At the same time, the population of the United States was increasing rapidly. More people would provide the labor supply for the production of goods, and the increasing population would provide the market for the sale of goods. People were moving to the western lands, and they were moving from towns to cities. There was a need for good roads to transport people, armies, and trade. Various states and sometimes cities assumed the responsibility of financing canal building and other transportation projects when the national government was unwilling to provide funding.

Westward emigration brought together people of diverse backgrounds. The pioneers of the West were hardy and self-reliant, and they were judged on what they could do, not on what they knew. They strongly believed in government for and of the people. Manhood suffrage was for all who qualified, without regard to social class, life work, or wealth.

In 1819 Missouri asked to join the Union. The population included some slave owners and about 10,000 slaves. At that time, there was an equal number of free and slave states, 11 each. Congress wanted to reject the admission if slavery were to be permitted in Missouri. There was a heated debate since the action taken in this case might set precedence for other states formed from the Louisiana Purchase. Fortunately, Maine requested admission into the Union about this time. In a compromise, the Senate admitted both states in 1820 in a single bill which also prohibited slavery in the Louisiana Territory in those states created north of the boundary set at the parallel 36°30′. The balance was maintained, at least temporarily. Maine entered as a free state and Missouri entered as a slave state. Major differences and hard feelings were developing between the North and South.

Another indication that the country was growing and strengthening was the Supreme Court. John Marshall, a Virginian, had been appointed Chief Justice in January of 1801. He held this office for 34 years. Decisions made by him and his associates were in support of federal authority against that of the states in many of the cases. For example, in *McCulloch v. Maryland*, the Court agreed that Congress had the right to establish a bank. Therefore, the state was prohibited from taxing the bank except for the ground and building it occupied.

After Florida was ceded to the United States in 1819, Spanish colonies in Latin America struggled for their independence. Henry Clay urged President Monroe to recognize the Latin American republics, but Secretary of State, John Quincy Adams, was cautious for a number of reasons. One reason was because the European powers had pledged themselves to help restore the former colonies to their mother countries. Finally, on May 4, 1822, President Monroe officially recognized the Spanish republics. In his annual message to Congress in December, 1823, Monroe announced the policy of the United States toward the territory and government of the American continent. European interference in Latin America would be regarded as an unfriendly act and a threat toward the United States. The United States had now stated publicly that they will defend the Western Hemisphere against any European interference. This "doctrine" has been referred to as "the cornerstone of American foreign policy."

General Andrew Jackson, Henry Clay, John Quincy Adams, and William H. Crawford ran for presidency in 1824. No candidate received the majority of the electoral votes required by the Constitution although Jackson had received most of the popular votes. The House of Representatives had to select from the three highest names on the list. Henry Clay was out of the race; he gave his support to Adams. The House selected Adams, and Adams immediately offered Clay a cabinet post. Jackson's supporters were furious. Jackson resigned from the Senate and began a four-year campaign against Adams.

Adams met with opposition all through his term. Rivalry existed between the three sections of the country. New England was a conservative region, socially and politically. The South supported slavery; and the pioneer West was independent and self-reliant. Adams held to the policy of a strong national government. Because of the diverse views and positions of members of Congress, he was unable to promote his programs.

Great Britain began exporting to the United States manufactured goods which had accumulated in its ports during the War of 1812 at low prices. The Tariff of 1816 was passed which continued the high duties levied for the war expenses in 1812 and even increased the rates by 15 percent to 20 percent. However, this tariff did not stop the flood of manufactured goods from Great Britain. In 1824 a new tariff raised the average duty from 20 percent to 36 percent. The major purpose of this tariff was to protect the prices of American goods against English competition where labor was cheaper and more abundant and the processes of manufacturing more advanced. The economy of the South was beginning to suffer. The South challenged the right of Congress to levy a protective tariff. Too, the population of the North was rapidly surpassing that of the South. The North would be represented by more legislators in Congress, thereby, having more power. The South felt bitter and used by the federal government and became defenders of states' rights.

"The Tariff of Abominations" was passed by Congress in 1828. It was resented by New England shipowners and southern planters who felt the tariffs to be unfair. It strengthened the position of the defenders of states' rights over federalism.

In the presidential election of 1828, Jackson's victory was overwhelming. His victory was hailed as a triumph for rugged and independent frontier settlers who believed in the right to govern themselves. He received the most popular and electoral votes. The new Democratic party was now in power.

INFLUENTIAL PERSONS IN GOVERNMENT

Match the descriptions in Column II with the persons they describe in Column I. There are two descriptors for each individual listed in Column I.

COLUMN I

_____ _____1. John Quincy Adams

_____ _____2. Thomas H. Benton

_____ _____3. John C. Calhoun

_____ _____4. Henry Clay

_____ _____5. DeWitt Clinton

_____ _____6. William H. Crawford

_____ _____7. Albert Gallatin

_____ _____8. Andrew Jackson

_____ _____9. Rufus King

_____ _____10. Daniel Webster

COLUMN II

a. "Hero of New Orleans"
b. Governor of New York State
c. Brilliant orator from Georgia
d. Helped build up the commonwealth of Tennessee
e. A Swiss by birth
f. Sixth president of the United States
g. South Carolinian with a passion for national expansion
h. Received college education at Dartmouth College
i. Son of a Federalist president
j. Senator from New York
k. Kentuckian and Speaker of the House during election of 1824
l. Supported the construction of Erie Canal
m. "Old Hickory"
n. Son of a New Hampshire farmer
o. Secretary of Treasury under Jefferson and Madison
p. During Monroe's presidency, he was an antislavery orator in Congress.
q. Born in North Carolina in 1782
r. Nearly defeated Monroe for the Republican nomination for the presidency in 1816
s. Forced Madison to declare war on Great Britain in 1812
t. Outstanding leader and orator

PRESIDENTIAL ELECTIONS

Study the table on Presidential Elections.
  A. List as many questions as you can that could be answered as one studies the table.
  B. List three questions that can only be partly answered by the table. Note what additional information is needed.
  C. What can you infer if you were given the following information regarding percentage of voter participation?
      Election of 1824: 26.9%; of 1828: 57.6%; and 1832: 55.4%

YEAR	CANDIDATES	PARTIES	POPULAR VOTE	ELECTORAL VOTE
1789	GEORGE WASHINGTON (VA)			69
	John Adams			34
	others			35
1792	GEORGE WASHINGTON (VA)			132
	John Adams			77
	George Clinton			50
	others			5
1796	JOHN ADAMS (MA)	Federalist		71
	Thomas Jefferson	Dem.-Rep.		68
	Thomas Pinckney	Federalist		59
	Aaron Burr	Dem.-Rep.		30
	others			48
1800	THOMAS JEFFERSON (VA)	Dem.-Rep.		73
	Aaron Burr	Dem.-Rep.		73
	John Adams	Federalist		65
	C. C. Pinckney	Federalist		64
	John Jay	Federalist		1
1804	THOMAS JEFFERSON (VA)	Dem.-Rep.		162
	C. C. Pinckney	Federalist		14
1808	JAMES MADISON (VA)	Dem.-Rep.		122
	C. C. Pinckney	Federalist		47
	George Clinton	Dem.-Rep.		6
1812	JAMES MADISON (VA)	Dem.-Rep.		128
	DeWitt Clinton	Federalist		89
1816	JAMES MONROE (VA)	Dem.-Rep.		183
	Rufus King	Federalist		34
1820	JAMES MONROE (VA)	Dem.-Rep.		321
	John Quincy Adams	Dem.-Rep.		1
1824	JOHN QUINCY ADAMS (MA)	Dem.-Rep.	108,740	84
	Andrew Jackson	Dem.-Rep.	153,544	99
	William H. Crawford	Dem.-Rep.	46,618	41
	Henry Clay	Dem.-Rep.	47,136	37
1828	ANDREW JACKSON (TN)	Democratic	647,286	178
	John Quincy Adams	National Rep.	508,064	83
1832	ANDREW JACKSON (TN)	Democratic.	687,502	219
	Henry Clay	National Rep.	530,189	49
	John Floyd	Independent		11
	William Wirt	Anti-Mason	33,108	7

SUGGESTED TEACHING ACTIVITIES

1. Topics for further study:
   a. tariffs
   b. Rufus King
   c. DeWitt Clinton
   d. Erie Canal
   e. "favorite sons"
   f. Florida
   g. statehood
   h. James Monroe
   i. Monroe Doctrine
   j. Missouri Compromise
   k. slavery
   l. John Marshall
   m. Henry Clay
   n. *Dartmouth v. Woodward*
   o. Washington Irving
   p. James Fenimore Cooper
   q. states' rights
   r. John Marshall
   s. railroads

2. Prepare a time line to include the following events:
   a. Death of John Adams
   b. Jackson's election to presidency
   c. Baltimore & Ohio Railroad begins operation
   d. Monroe Doctrine is announced
   e. Death of Thomas Jefferson
   f. Erie Canal opens
   g. Missouri Compromise
   h. "Tariff of Abominations" passes
   i. Cyrus McCormick invents reaper
   j. Creek Indians cede lands to Georgia
   k. John Quincy Adams becomes president
   l. Spain cedes Florida to United States

3. Class Discussion: What are tariffs? Duties? What is a protective tariff? Why was the Tariff of 1828 called the Tariff of Abominations? What section of the country—North, South, or West—would like to see high duties on manufactured woolens? Why? Who would like low or no duty on raw wool? Why? Do you think it was possible to put duties on items without antagonizing New England manufacturers, the Ohio sheep herders, the cotton planters in the South, and the miners in Pennsylvania? Do you think the automobile manufacturers today would like to see high duties on imported automobiles? Why? Would the buyers agree with the manufacturers? Why or why not? Do you think that a protective tariff is sometimes a good thing? Why or why not?

4. Ask student volunteers to bring their guitars or any other instrument to play while their classmates learn and sing selections from "Songs of Early America" and "Frontier Songs of Work and Play." These are found in *The American Heritage Songbook* (New York: American Heritage Publishing Company, Inc., 1969.)

Suggestions for Supplementary Reading:

Franck, Irene M. and David M. Brownstone. *The American Way West.* Adapted from *To the Ends of the Earth.* New York: Facts on File, 1991.

Paletta, LuAnn. *The World Almanac of First Ladies.* New York: World Almanac, A Scripps Howard Company, 1990.

Smith, Carter. (Editor). *The Legendary Wild West: A Sourcebook on the American West.* Brookfield, Connecticut: The Millbrook Press, 1992.

Stein, R. Conrad. *The Story of the Erie Canal.* Illustrated by Keith Neely. Chicago: Children's Press, 1985.

Highlights in American History

THE ERA OF JACKSONIAN DEMOCRACY

When the architects of the Constitution were structuring the United States government, they were concerned that it not resemble that of England with a strong executive or king. Even though a position of president was created, nevertheless, considerable power was delegated to Congress, especially the Senate. President Andrew Jackson regarded himself as the champion of the American people and protector of the people from the "corrupt politicians" who had denied him the presidency four years ago. He was a domineering man of strong will; anyone who opposed him was regarded as an enemy. He was inconsistent in what he said and what he did. He advised against a second presidential term, yet he served a second term. He ignored his official cabinet in favor of unofficial advisors called the "kitchen cabinet."

People engaged in invention and industry helped to shape the course of history during the time of President Andrew Jackson. The production of crops on farms increased and goods were produced in efficient ways in factories with machines. Steamboats, steam locomotives, and better roads improved transportation and stimulated travel and business in every direction. Workers were demanding higher wages, shorter hours of work, more sanitary and safe conditions in shops and factories, and free schools for their children.

Far reaching political changes, too, were in progress during the 1830s and 1840s. All social and economic classes of people participated actively in government. States began to extend voting rights and to shorten terms of offices. The people voted directly for many public officials and judges for the first time. National conventions for nominating candidates of each party for president and vice-president and for publishing a "platform" developed during this time. At first each state had one vote in the selection of the candidates. Later each state was represented by a number of delegates twice as large as its representation in Congress.

In 1830 tariff was a major concern. President Jackson, a slave owner and Southerner, declared that Congress had the right to levy a protective tariff; it was a desirable policy. In the Senate, a proposal was introduced that public lands should not be sold for awhile. Some senators felt that Eastern merchants, who wanted high duties to protect their products, also wanted to stop the migration West of cheap laborers from their factories. The discussion in the Senate led to the question of states' rights. Daniel Webster, responding to Senator Robert Y. Hayne in the famous debate, emphasized that the people had created the government, not the states. "It is a people's government, made for the people, made by the people, answerable to the people." Webster ended his dramatic speech with, "Liberty and Union, now and forever, one and inseparable."

A new tariff bill was passed in 1832 with slightly lower rates; it was still highly protective. The Southern members of Congress met in November, 1832 and declared the tariff acts of 1828 and 1832 "null, void, and no law." South Carolinians were ordered to pay no duties under these laws after February 1, 1833. If the federal government enforced the laws, the states would secede from the Union. Senators John C. Calhoun and Henry Clay worked together to develop a compromise. The duties were to be reduced gradually until 1842 when they should reach the level of the Tariff Act of 1816. The Compromise Tariff was enacted into law in March, 1833. At the same time, a "Force Bill" was passed which gave the president the right to send the army and navy of the United States to collect the duties in South Carolina.

By 1830, the government was forcing the Indians to move to reservations in Oklahoma. When the Supreme Court ruled that the government had no right to remove the Indians from their lands, President Jackson ignored the decision. The Indians left reluctantly or fought to stay. Thousands of Cherokee were marched from their homes to Oklahoma forcibly by the American Army. Many of them died on the trip, "The Trail of Tears," from disease and starvation.

Andrew Jackson became president a second time. He felt strongly that the government should not recharter the National Bank because it was contrary to the principles of democracy. Jackson vetoed the bill to renew the charter of the National Bank because he believed it was a dangerous monopoly managed by affluent citizens for their own wealth. Secretary of the Treasury Taney was instructed to place the federal revenues in certain state banks, called "pet banks." These "wildcat" banks issued notes far beyond the legitimate business needs of the country and far beyond their real capital in gold and silver.

In 1836, President Jackson issued his famous Specie Circular, forbidding the Treasury of the United States to accept any money but gold and silver (specie) in payment for further sales of public land. This led to the Panic of 1837. The "wildcat" banks did not have the gold and silver for the notes they had issued. Building projects ceased, and people lost their jobs. Banks closed and American credit abroad was almost ruined. It took almost six years before the country recovered from this economic depression. The government did not deposit its monies in the National Bank or the "pet banks" of the states. A system of government deposit was adopted under Van Buren's presidency which completely separated public funds from the banking business.

Because of his autocratic and unbending conduct, Jackson had many enemies. The opponents of "King Andrew" formed a party and called themselves the Whigs. In the election of 1836, Martin Van Buren became the next president, Jackson's personal choice for president. Van Buren was an able politician but he failed to hold the Democratic party together and he was blamed for the Panic of 1837. The Whigs nominated William Henry Harrison of Ohio—a frontiersman, Indian fighter, and hero of the War of 1812. He was elected; however, he died shortly after his inauguration and John Tyler became president. Harrison's victory marked the end of Andrew Jackson's era. The sectional interests between the North and South were becoming more pronounced and divisive on economic and slavery issues.

RECEPTION FOR THE PEOPLE'S PRESIDENT

Many historians consider Andrew Jackson the first popularly elected President and one of the great presidents of the United States. People regarded him as "their own President." President Jackson firmly believed that the President was a direct representative of the people. As President he emerged as a leader of a powerful and rising democratic movement, bringing social, economic, and political changes to all aspects of life in this country.

The day of Jackson's inaugural, March 4th, 1829, was cloudy and cool. The sun, though, broke through the skies when Jackson left for the inaugural ceremonies at the Capitol. At that time, he was grief-stricken because of the recent loss of his wife, Rachel. He, himself, was in poor health. Nevertheless, he appeared a dignified and grand presidential figures. The President-Elect was over six feet tall, wearing a plain black suit and a black cravat without a hat covering his thick, white hair. A noisy and proud crowd awaited his inaugural address.

After the program, people wanted to touch him. The police were unable to maintain any order. Jackson, with the help of friends, finally left on horseback for the reception at the White House. According to custom, after the inaugural program, arrangements are made to entertain selected guests. Long, beautiful tables were spread with cakes, ice cream, and orange punch. Again, police control proved inadequate. The crowd that followed the President up the Avenue entered the White House through doors or through windows. The reception rooms were extremely crowded. Guests, with or without invitations, continued to come. The President, after being pushed around for an hour, willingly left the reception.

Finally, someone removed the punch bowls to the lawn of the White House. This relieved some of the congestion in the reception rooms. When the reception was over, some individuals described the White House as resembling a "pigsty." China was broken, and many guests were disheveled from the crowded and unmanageable conditions. It was, indeed, a memorable inauguration for President Jackson.

1. Why do you think President Jackson is regarded as one of the "great" Presidents?

   _____

   _____

2. Place yourself in the position of someone who attended the inaugural ceremony and the reception for President Jackson. How would you describe the exciting day to your family when you returned to the farm?

   _____

   _____

   _____

   _____

IDENTIFYING NICKNAMES

Match the following nicknames with the individuals listed below and in one or two sentences tell why the name(s) was given to that individual. Some individuals have more than one nickname.

a. Czar Nicholas   e. Little Magician   i. Old Tippecanoe
b. King Andrew I   f. Sage of Kinderhood   j. Red Fox
c. Harry of the West   g. Great Debater   k. War Hawk
d. Great Pacificator   h. Old Hickory

_____1. President Andrew Jackson _____

_____

_____

_____2. President Martin Van Buren _____

_____

_____

_____3. President William H. Harrison _____

_____

_____

_____4. Senator Henry Clay_____

_____

_____

_____5. Senator John C. Calhoun _____

_____

_____

_____6. Senator Daniel Webster _____

_____

_____

_____7. Nicholas Biddle _____

_____

_____

SUGGESTED TEACHING ACTIVITIES

1. Topics for further study:
   - a. Alexis de Tocqueville
   - b. spoils system
   - c. Dorr Rebellion
   - d. nullification
   - e. "Kitchen Cabinet"
   - f. Rachel Jackson
   - g. John Tyler
   - h. Peggy Eaton Affair
   - i. Webster-Hayne Debate
   - j. George Catlin
   - k. Trail of Tears
   - l. Five Civilized Nations
   - m. Nicholas Biddle
   - n. Andrew Jackson
   - o. John C. Calhoun
   - p. Henry Clay
   - q. Daniel Webster
   - r. William H. Harrison
   - s. Martin Van Buren
   - t. Webster-Ashburton Treaty

2. Assign students to arrange the following statements according to what happened first, second, etc.
   - A. Jackson vetoed the bill to renew the Bank's charter.
   - B. Jackson won the election of 1828.
   - C. The Bank closed its doors.
   - D. Jackson was overhwelmingly reelected in 1832.
   - E. The Second Bank was chartered by the United States government.
   - F. Congress voted to renew the Bank's charter.

3. Assign students to prepare special independent studies and to share their findings with the class in the form of an oral report, panel discussion, and/or bulletin board display.
   - a. Political Parties during the 1820s and 1830s
   - b. Voting rights during the 1820s and 1830s
   - c. Electoral College
   - d. Popular Elections

4. Plan a visit to an art museum and have students prepare a list of paintings that show people and life during the 1830s and 1840s. What are the themes of most of the paintings? Are any of the notable persons of the period in the paintings? Which ones? Why do you think the artist used them as subjects in the paintings?

5. Assign students to list the names of streets, cities, and buildings that are named after the notable persons who participated in government service during the 1830s and 1840s.

6. The "Great Triumvirate" included three outstanding men: John C. Calhoun, Henry Clay, and Daniel Webster. All three aspired for the presidency. Prepare a list of the accomplishments and beliefs of these men on the chalkboard and discuss the similarities and differences among them. Why do you think they never became president?

Suggestions for Supplementary Reading:

Andrist, Ralph K. *Andrew Jackson: Soldier and Statesman*. New York: American Heritage Publishing Company, Inc., 1963.

Bleeker, Sonia. *The Cherokee: Indians of the Mountains*. New York: William Morrow & Company, 1952.

THE ABOLITIONISTS AND SLAVERY

Slaves were imported to the American colonies to work in the tobacco, indigo, and rice fields or as household servants in the South. Thousands of slaves were brought in the years before and after the independence of the United States. After the invention of the cotton gin in 1793, more slaves were needed as the demand for cotton increased. The slave trade made many ship owners and investors wealthy in England and in the colonies. The Southern planters found slavery economically profitable and the basis of a social order in which they enjoyed a comfortable and powerful position.

Slavery was a part of the triangular trade. The British and colonial ship owners, in the first leg of the triangle, took rum made in New England to Africa. There the ship owners bartered the rum for slaves. Then, the black slaves were taken by ship, the next leg of the triangle, to the West Indies in exchange for sugar and molasses. The last leg of the triangle involved taking the sugar and molasses to New England to make more rum. The black slaves were chained together in gangs and packed closely in the unbearable and unsanitary holds of the ships. They were brutally treated and many died on the ships.

As stated in the Constitution, three-fifths of the slaves were counted in the population in making up the census for the House of Representatives. Furthermore, Congress was prohibited from discontinuing the slave trade for 20 years. A few people were dissatisfied with these items in the Constitution and petitioned Congress to abolish slavery. However, they met with failure since Congress refused to make it a concern of the federal government. It was a "domestic institution"; therefore, subject to the laws of the states not the federal government. Congress imposed a tax of $10 per head on imported slaves; this was authorized by the Constitution.

Congress appeared to support the cause of slavery. In 1792 Kentucky was admitted to the Union with a state constitution which upheld slavery. In 1793 Congress passed a fugitive slave law which permitted a slave owner to reclaim a runaway black in any state in the Union by a mere decision of the local judge, without jury trial. In 1796 Congress promised North Carolina that its lands west of the Alleghenies would not prohibit slavery. In 1798 slavery was permitted by Congress in the Mississippi territory. In 1803 slavery was protected in the Louisiana Territory wherever it already existed. In 1805 Congress defeated a bill to free slaves in the District of Columbia and in 1812 Louisiana was admitted as a slave state. When Missouri petitioned for statehood as a slave state, a compromise was finally reached when Maine asked for admittance as a free state in 1820.

The debates about Missouri's statehood emphasized the ethical aspects of the slavery question. People against slavery, abolitionists, insisted that its practice denied human rights and was not in keeping with the principles of the Declaration of Independence. It was wrong for one human being to own another human being. The South justified the practice of slavery on social and economic reasons. Those who defended slavery believed that it actually benefited blacks. They also argued that textile factory owners and consumers in the North who purchased the cotton and sold and bought manufactured cotton products benefited from the use of slaves on the plantations. Furthermore, they accused the Northerners of encouraging the slaves to rebel against their owners.

When the issue of slavery was debated in Congress, Benjamin Lundy, a New Jersey Quaker, began to publish a weekly periodical devoted to the cause of the abolition of slavery. He traveled to different states speaking to church and college groups and forming antislavery societies wherever he went. On a visit to Boston in 1828, he met William Lloyd Garrison who strongly believed that slavery was sinful; he was an uncompromising abolitionist who demanded an end to slavery. Garrison also began to publish an anti-slavery newspaper, *The Liberator*, which was read by many people. Frederick Douglass, a black, was an outstanding orator and leader in advancing the antislavery cause. *Uncle Tom's Cabin*, a novel authored by Harriet Beecher Stowe, became a powerful and widely read abolitionist work of fiction. Southern planters wanted censorship of the press and of the public platform to silence antislavery agitation. In the North there was also hostility against the abolitionists. W. Lloyd Garrison was almost tarred and feathered by the citizens of Boston. Luckily, he was rescued by the police and put in prison for safety. These abolitionists worked hard to inform the citizens of the issues involved in slavery. Oftentimes, they did not realize how effective they were. Today, Americans can see the success of their work.

The more practical abolitionists formed a political party, the Liberty Party which called for an end to slavery. The political party attempted to solve the problem of slavery according to the procedures and processes recognized in the Constitution. They nominated James G. Birney, a Southerner who had converted to the abolitionist cause, as candidate for president in the election of 1840. Even though the presidency was won by William H. Harrison, a Whig, the Liberty Party greatly influenced attitudes and ideas about slavery during the 1840s and 1850s.

Slavery was contrary to the principles of human equality, human worth, and human dignity. The work of reformers such as abolitionists and antislavery advocates tried to draw the people's attention to the seriousness of the slavery issue. Yet, attempts to rid slavery through plans for gradual emancipation were not successful. Instead laws were passed to fix the status of slavery on blacks forever, and these laws and attitudes eventually led to revolution and bloodshed.

SUPPORTING AND ABOLISHING SLAVERY IN THE 1850s

Complete the chart below:

REASONS FOR SUPPORTING SLAVERY	REASONS FOR ABOLISHING SLAVERY

ORGANIZING DATA

Answer the question after each table.

TABLE I

LINE STATE	DATE OF ADMITTANCE	CAPITAL	SLAVE/FREE
1. Missouri	1821	Jefferson City	Free
2. Maine	1803	Augusta	Free
3. Alabama	1819	Montgomery	Slave
4. Ohio	1820	Columbus	Free

A. Which lines are incorrect?_____ Make them correct.

TABLE II

LINE	TERM	DEFINITION
1.	*emancipation*	stood for keeping slavery out of the territories
2.	*abolitionism*	movement to end slavery in the United States
3.	*slavery*	system in which people are owned by other people
4.	*Liberty Party*	act of freeing the slaves

B. Which lines are incorrect?_____ Make them correct.

TABLE III

LINE AUTHOR/EDITOR	LITERATURE NOVEL/NEWSPAPER	DATE OF PUBLICATION
1. James Fenimore Cooper	*The Last of the Mohicans*	1826
2. William Lloyd Garrison	*The Liberator*	Began in 1831
3. Frederick Douglass	*Uncle Tom's Cabin*	1852
4. Harriet Beecher Stowe	*Narrative of the Life of Frederick Douglass*	1845

C. Which lines are incorrect?_____ Make them correct.

SUGGESTED TEACHING ACTIVITIES

1. Topics for further study:
   - a. triangular trade
   - b. Fugitive Slave Act
   - c. Harriet Beecher Stowe
   - d. *Uncle Tom's Cabin*
   - e. Benjamin Lundy
   - f. Frederick Douglass
   - g. William Lloyd Garrison
   - h. Benjamin Lundy
   - i. James C. Birney
   - j. Elijah Lovejoy
   - k. King Cotton
   - l. Liberty Party
   - m. abolitionists
   - n. David Walker

2. Duplicate the following table on the chalkboard which shows membership in the House of Representatives between 1800 and 1850.

Year	Total Membership	Members from Free States	Members from Slave States
1800	141	76	65
1810	175	96	79
1820	213	123	90
1830	240	141	99
1840	223	135	88
1850	232	142	90

Questions for discussion: Why is the total membership in the House increasing? In 1800, how many of the states were free states? Slave states? Why are there more representatives from the free states than from the slave states? Are the percentages of members from the slave states increasing or decreasing? Explain. How many states were in the Union in 1850? How many were slave states? Free states? How many members were in the Senate during this period of time? How was equal power maintained in the Senate?

3. Read to students selected excerpts from Alex Haley's *Roots* (New York: Doubleday & Company, Inc., 1976). As a class, view the video on *Roots*. Class discussion should include the African culture, the conditions on the ship, life on the plantation, and American principles of human equality.

4. If there is a university nearby, a specialist in black history might be invited to speak to the class about slavery and its effects on those enslaved.

5. Read to students selected excerpts from Harriet Beecher Stowe's *Uncle Tom's Cabin*. New York: New American Library, 1966. Discuss culture of blacks, principle of inequality, and abolitionists.

Suggestions for Supplementary Reading:

Ingraham, Leonard W. *Slavery in the United States*. New York: Franklin Watts, Inc., 1968.

McKissack, Patricia and Fredrick. *Frederick Douglass: The Black Lion*. Chicago: Children's Press, 1970.

Ofosu-Appiah, L. H. *People in Bondage: African Slavery in the Modern Era*. Minneapolis, MN: Lerner Publications Company, 1971,

Wise, Winifred E. *Harriet Beecher Stowe: Woman With a Cause*. New York: G. P. Putnam's Sons, 1965.

WESTWARD EXPANSION

Westward expansion was characterized by a number of distinct migrations. The first occurred when the French were driven out of North America in 1763. The second migration took place after the War of 1812 when five new states were added to the Union. The third and most dramatic migration extended the boundary of the United States to the Pacific Ocean. There was some opposition to expansion from the original states because they did not want to assume the burden of defending and developing the new territories. After the debates over the Missouri Compromise and the abolitionist agitation, the acquisition of new territory in the West or the admission of new states was marked with heated discussion of the slavery issue.

In 1818 Great Britain agreed to share with the United States for 10 years the Oregon country, lying beyond the Rocky Mountains, between 42° and 54° 40′ north latitude. The agreement was considered fair; both countries had claims on Oregon, based upon exploration and settlement. This agreement was renewed. In 1832 settlers bravely traveled the dangerous trail to Oregon by wagon trains and founded their homes on picturesque and fertile lands. Dr. Marcus Whitman and his wife established a mission and encouraged other settlements in Oregon. By 1845, there were about 5,000 settlers in Oregon. In the election of 1844, some of the campaign slogans of the Democratic party were "54°40′ or fight!" and "All of Oregon or Nothing." Great Britain did not want war over Oregon, and too, the fur trade was not as profitable as it had been. Therefore, in 1846, it was agreed that 49° north latitude would serve as the boundary between the United States and Canada all the way to the Pacific Ocean. Oregon Territory was established in 1848 by Congress as a part of the United States.

There was also expansion on the southern borders in Texas. Mexico had gained its independence from Spain in 1821. Americans had been crossing the Sabine River into Texas, Mexican territory, for many years. By 1830, there were nearly 20,000 Americans in Texas. At first the Americans were welcomed. They were given large tracts of land if they promised to become Roman Catholics and obey the laws of Mexico. Slavery was illegal in Mexico, yet Americans used slaves on their plantations to care for their cotton. The weak Mexican government did not enforce its laws; therefore, there was no conflict between the Americans and the Mexicans. When Antonio Lopez de Santa Anna became Mexico's new president in 1832, he decided to enforce its laws regarding slavery and religion and prohibited further American migration into Mexico. When Santa Anna's army moved into Texas, the Texans declared their independence. After a devastating battle at the Alamo, a mission in San Antonio, Santa Anna emerged victorious, believing the rebellion was crushed.

The Texan army, led by General Sam Houston, initiated a surprise attack on Santa Anna in San Jacinto in 1836. This battle ended quickly with a Texan victory and Santa Anna promised to recognize Texan independence. A republic was set up with General Sam Houston as president and a constitution was adopted. Slavery was permitted but the importation of slaves from any place except the United States was forbidden. Most of the Texans were in favor of annexing Texas to the United States. However, if the United States accepted Texas, they would need the consent of Mexico, which refused to recognize independence of Texas. This might mean war with Mexico. Furthermore, this was not the time to add Texas, a slave territory, to the Union; the balance between slave and free states had to be held in check. Eventually, because of British influence in Texas and other political issues, Texas officially became a state in 1845.

Mexico refused to recognize the annexation of Texas. President Polk sent John Slidell of Louisiana to Mexico in 1845 to adjust any differences over the Texan claims. The Mexican government refused to recognize him and dismissed him from the country in August, 1846. President Polk ordered General Zachary Taylor to move to the Rio Grande River and to fortify a position on the northern bank. When General Taylor refused to retreat to the Nueces River, the Mexican commander crossed the Rio Grande and ambushed the American troops. When President Polk was notified of the attack, he sent a special message to Congress requesting war with Mexico. Congress declared war on Mexico in 1846.

General Taylor, "Old Rough and Ready," was ordered to cross the Rio Grande River and occupy northeastern Mexico. This was a successful strategy. Colonel Stephen W. Kearny marched to Santa Fe and took that town with no opposition. When the Californians heard about the war against Mexico, they immediately declared their independence from Mexico. With the help of Colonel Kearny and the United States army, the conquest of California was completed in 1846 with little conflict. In spite of these American successes, Mexico refused to agree to peace or to give up the conquered territory.

President Polk then ordered the American forces to strike at the heart of Mexico by sending General Winfield Scott to fight his way to Mexico City. General Santa Anna and his army attacked General Taylor's troops at Buena Vista in 1847. The Mexicans were defeated. General Scott's troops finally reached Mexico City and there met no resistance. A new Mexican government was now in power, and they were willing to discuss terms of peace. The Treaty of Guadalupe Hidalgo was concluded on February 2, 1848. Mexico agreed to cede California and New Mexico to the United States and recognize the Rio Grande River as the boundary of Texas. In return the United States assumed the claims of its citizens against Mexico and agreed to pay $15 million to the Mexicans. President Polk wanted more land from Mexico and the antislavery people thought the acquisition of Mexico was a plot to extend slavery. The treaty, nevertheless, was approved in the senate and the Mexican War, an unpopular war, was over.

More than a million square miles of new territory were added to the United States during the 1840s. Growth in population and a prosperous and growing economy created optimism and a desire for adventure. This led to expansion and dramatic changes in living.

MAP STUDY

List on the back of this map the territories which were acquired by the United States from 1783 until 1853. In two or three sentences tell how each territory was acquired. Then, on the map below, draw in the lines and identify all of the territories acquired by the United States from 1783 until 1853.

Name_____

ANALYZING THE MEXICAN WAR

After studying about the Mexican War, complete the following questions:

1. When did it occur?

    _____

    _____

2. Where did it occur?

    _____

    _____

3. Who was involved?

    _____

    _____

4. Why were they involved?

    _____

    _____

    _____

    _____

5. What was the outcome?

    _____

    _____

    _____

    _____

6. Do you think the Mexican War could have been prevented? Explain.

    _____

    _____

    _____

    _____

SUGGESTED TEACHING ACTIVITIES

1. Topics for further study:
   - a. Santa Anna
   - b. Currier & Ives
   - c. Marcus Whitman
   - d. Oregon Trail
   - e. James K. Polk
   - f. Charles Russell
   - g. John Tyler
   - h. Stephen Austin
   - i. Davy Crockett
   - j. Alamo Mission
   - k. Sam Houston
   - l. Frederic Remington
   - m. Zachary Taylor
   - n. Titian Peale
   - o. James Audubon
   - p. George Catlin
   - q. John A. Sutter
   - r. Stephen W. Kearny
   - s. Winfield Scott

2. Assign students to prepare an automobile trip to the Pacific Ocean, following the Oregon Trail as closely as possible. What landmarks will you see that were identified by the early settlers? How difficult do you think the trip was for the early settlers? Why? How does the trip of the settlers compare to your trip? The AAA travel office and/or the Oregon Travel Bureau may be helpful in providing you with maps and information.

3. Have students imagine that they are members of the Cheyenne tribe and see a wagon train with a hundred families traveling west. Assign them to write a short paragraph telling how they might have felt and reacted to the scene.

4. Have students imagine that they are reporters for a New York newspaper in San Antonio witnessing first-hand the battle of the Alamo. Assign them to write an article of what they observe for their readers.

5. Have students imagine that they are living in Columbus, Ohio and they are thinking about leaving home for the West in the 1840s. Where will they go? Why? What route will they take? What will they take with them?

6. Map Study: On a map of the United States have students locate the Oregon Trail, Santa Fe Trail, The Alamo, Santa Fe, St. Louis, Sabine River, Nueces River, Pecos River, Salt Lake City, Sutter's Fort, Kansas City, and Seattle.

7. Student volunteers may create a mural to display in the classroom illustrating the different scenes one may have seen as the settlers, adventurers, missionaries, and soldiers moved westward.

8. Make a time line for the classroom. Include events such as: Gadsden Purchase, Texas independence from Mexico, invention of cotton gin, California Gold Rush, Texas statehood, Mexican War, Treaty of Guadalupe Hidalgo, election of Zachary Taylor as president.

Suggestions for Supplementary Reading:

Eaton, Jeanette. *Narcissa Whitman: Pioneer of Oregon*. New York: Harcourt, Brace and Company, 1941.

Hoyt. Edwin P. *Zachary Taylor*. Chicago: Reilly & Lee Company, 1966.

Smith, Carter. ed. *The Legendary Wild West: A Sourcebook on the American West*. Brookfield, Connecticut, The Millbrook Press, 1992.

THE APPROACHING CRISIS OF DISUNION

During the winter of 1849-1850, the governmental leaders of the United States tried to bring about a compromise on the slavery issue to all sections of the country. Henry Clay upheld the Union and proposed (1) that California should enter the Union as a free state; (2) that in the rest of the Mexican cession, territorial governments should be formed without restrictions as to slavery; (3) that Texas should yield in its boundary dispute with New Mexico and the federal government should assume its public debt; (4) that the slave trade, but not slavery itself, should be abolished in the District of Columbia; and (5) that a more effective fugitive slave law should be enacted.

Many fine speeches were made in the Senate during the debates concerning these proposals. Henry Clay, a prominent speaker, was a strong advocate for harmony. John C. Calhoun, old and ill, spoke out for states' rights and against federal interference with slavery. Daniel Webster, against the extension of slavery into new territory, favored Clay's compromise measures.

In July, President Taylor died suddenly and Vice-President Millard Fillmore, who supported the compromise, succeeded him. With the aid of legislators such as Stephen A. Douglas and William H. Seward, it was finally passed and signed by the president in August. The Northerners found it difficult to accept the Fugitive Slave Act. The runaway slave, a fugitive, was not allowed a trial nor to testify in his/her own behalf. This act guaranteed the protection of slave property in every part of the United States by making every citizen involved in returning a fugitive to his/her master. Some states refused to obey this law by developing a system known as the "underground railroad," which provided escaped slaves with food and shelter as they tried to find their way to freedom in Canada. In secrecy, sympathetic Northerners permitted the use of their homes and barns as "stations" for escaping slaves.

The early 1850s were a time of great prosperity. Industrial and agricultural productions increased, gold and silver were discovered in California, the merchant marine fleet was growing, and greatly increased railroad mileage provided connections between all parts of the country. The demand for cotton convinced Southerners that slavery was the basis for their wealth. Laborers were needed in the factories and on the farms. Political revolts and economic hardships experienced by the Irish, Germans, and Chinese led many of them to come to this land of freedom and greater opportunity.

In 1854, Senator Douglas, the "Little Giant," introduced the Kansas-Nebraska Bill in Congress for the organization of the two territories on the principle of "squatter sovereignty." This meant that the voters within each area could decide whether to become a free or a slave state. The Bill was passed in 1854. As a consequence, resistance to the Fugitive Slave Law became even greater. The passage of this bill also led to the formation of a new political party at Jackson, Michigan. This powerful party, the Republican Party, demanded the repeal of the Kansas-Nebraska Act and of the Fugitive Slave Law of 1850 and resolved to work until slavery was eliminated.

While the bill was being debated, New Englanders formed a group to lead companies of emigrants to the new territories. They provided settlers with loans and helped with building homes and farming. The Southerners and citizens of Missouri were angered because they felt that the New Englanders were trying to prevent a fair and natural settlement of Kansas. Voting was fraudulent; two governments were organized, each charging the other with fraud and violence. In 1856 the Missourians attacked the town of Lawrence, burning the homes and public buildings. For revenge, John Brown led a determined group of anti-slavery men to a pro-slavery settlement and killed five men. President Pierce tried to ignore "Bleeding Kansas"; however, action had to be taken and he sided with the pro-slavery forces.

The Republican Convention adopted a platform which stated that it was "both the right and the duty of Congress" to prohibit slavery in the territories and selected John C. Fremont as their candidate for president. "Free speech, free press, free soil, Fre-mont and Victory!" However, the election of 1856 brought about the victory of James Buchanan of Pennsylvania, a Democrat. Even though the Republicans lost, they made a remarkable fight.

Anti-slavery citizens were again aroused when the Supreme Court announced its decision in the Dred Scott case in 1857. Dred Scott, a slave belonging to a man in Missouri, had been taken by his master into free territory and brought back again to Missouri. Years later, he sued his master's widow for his freedom on the ground that residence in a free territory had emancipated him. Chief Justice of the Supreme Court, Roger B. Taney, declared that the slave was not a citizen, only white men were citizens. The slave, therefore, could not sue in a court of the United States; he was the property of his owner.

In the summer of 1858, Senator Douglas returned to Illinois to begin his campaign for reelection. His Republican rival was Abraham Lincoln. Lincoln challenged Douglas to a series of debates on the merits of the Democratic doctrine of popular sovereignty in the territories and the Republican doctrine of the control of slavery in the territories by Congress. Seven remarkable debates took place. Douglas won the senatorship by the narrow margin of eight votes.

John Brown and his men, in October, 1859, seized the United States arsenal at Harper's Ferry in Virginia, raided the homes of planters, and freed about 30 slaves. The U. S. marines easily captured Brown, who was then tried for treason by the laws of Virginia and sentenced to death by hanging.

Shortly after this incident, the Republicans met in Chicago in May, 1860 and nominated Abraham Lincoln of Illinois for president. In the November, 1860 election, Lincoln carried all the Northern states except New Jersey and became the sixteenth president of the United States.

PEOPLE AND THEIR ACHIEVEMENTS

Match the persons listed in Column I with their achievements in Column II.

Column I

_____1. Dred Scott

_____2. Stephen A. Douglas

_____3. Henry Clay

_____4. Zachary Taylor

_____5. John C. Calhoun

_____6. Daniel Webster

_____7. Charles Sumner

_____8. John Brown

_____9. Harriet Tubman

_____10. Roger Taney

Column II

A. An anti-slavery citizen who decided he would invade the South, arm the slaves, and let them fight for their freedom. He was captured, tried for treason, and hanged.

B. Chief Justice of the Supreme Court who handed down the decision in the Dred Scott case that a free black was not a citizen and did not have the rights of a citizen in the United States.

C. An escaped slave who helped hundreds of other slaves escape successfully to freedom.

D. A senator from Kentucky who introduced the Compromise of 1850.

E. A professional soldier with no previous political experience who opposed the Compromise of 1850. He died suddenly while in an elected office in 1850.

F. A senator who was known as "the Little Giant." He and Abraham Lincoln were engaged in a series of debates on critical national issues.

G. A slave who sued for freedom because he resided for a period of time with his master in a free state and territory.

H. A powerful orator with a deep commitment to the cause of civil rights. After he presented his speech, "Crime Against Kansas," he was almost beaten to death. It took him over three years to recover from this assault.

I. A senator from Massachusetts who supported the Compromise of 1850.

J. A senator from South Carolina who attacked the Compromise of 1850 and demanded that the Northerners stop their attempts to limit slavery in the United States.

MAKING CONNECTIONS

Explain in two sentences all of the ways in which Column I is connected to corresponding item in Column II.

Column I		Column II
1. Compromise of 1850	_____	Henry Clay
2. Stephen A. Douglas	_____	Abraham Lincoln
3. John Brown	_____	Harper's Ferry
4. Underground Railroad	_____	Fugitive Slave Law
5. Cotton	_____	Slavery
6. Daniel Webster	_____	John C. Calhoun
7. Dred Scott	_____	Roger Taney
8. Kansas-Nebraska Act	_____	Bleeding Kansas

1. Topics for further study:
    a. Underground Railroad
    b. John C. Calhoun
    c. Daniel Webster
    d. Zachary Taylor
    e. Millard Fillmore
    f. Stephen A. Douglas
    g. William H. Seward
    h. Fugitive Slave Law
    i. "Bleeding Kansas"
    j. James Buchanan
    k. John C. Fremont
    l. Dred Scott case
    m. Charles Sumner
    n. Lincoln/Douglas Debates
    o. Harper's Ferry
    p. Republicans
    q. Henry Clay
    r. cotton
    s. popular sovereignty
    t. John Brown

2. Map Study: Make a map of the United States and identify all of the states and their capitals which were admitted to the Union by 1860 and note whether they are free or slave states. What inferences can you make regarding the conflict between the North and South over the slavery issue? Explain.

3. Have students pretend they are slaves and have just escaped with their mothers and/or fathers from a cotton plantation in Georgia. Have them write the story of their experiences as they avoid the U. S. marshals and pro-slavery citizens in their escape to freedom. The composition should include comments about their feelings and the people they met, their transportation facilities, sleeping accommodations, and food.

4. The growing of cotton made the economy of the South wealthy and prosperous and resulted in an increase in the number of slaves needed to work in the fields. In 1820 about 500,000 bales of cotton were picked, and in 1850 it had increased to 3,000,000 bales of cotton. Make a bar graph using the following information.

Slave Population from 1800 to 1860

Year	Total Population	Year	Total Population
1800	893,602	1840	2,487,355
1810	1,191,362	1850	3,204,313
1820	1,538,022	1860	3,953,760
1830	2,009,043		

What inferences can you make about the slave population and the economic prosperity in the South? How did the Northerners regard this increase in population?

Suggestions for Supplementary Reading:
Fritz, Jean. *Brady*. New York: Coward-McCann, Inc., 1960.
Jacob, Helen Pierce. *The Secret of the Strawbridge Place*. New York: Atheneum, 1976.
Nolan, Jeannette Covert. *John Brown*. New York: Julian Messner, Inc., 1950.
Sandburg, Carl. *Abe Lincoln Grows Up*. New York: Harcourt, Brace and Company, 1926.
Sterling, Dorothy. *Freedom Train: The Story of Harriet Tubman*. New York; Doubleday & Company, Inc., 1954.

Answer Key

STUDYING OUR HERITAGE

Why Should We Study Our Heritage?   Page 3
Responses will vary.

Studying About People and Events   Page 4
Responses will vary.

Who Are the Social Scientists?   Page 5
Responses will vary.

THE VOYAGE OF CHANGE

Columbus Crosses the Ocean   Page 8
1. Responses will vary.
2. It was named after a Florentine merchant, Amerigo Vespucci, who wrote a number of very colorful descriptions of his trip to the New World on a Portuguese expedition.
3. Map Study–Not all of Columbus's ships returned: *Santa Maria* was shipwrecked and the men on the *Pinta* deserted him.
4. Responses will vary.

Interpreting the Story of Columbus   Page 9
1. Columbus discovered a new continent.
2. He received financial assistance from Spanish rulers and sailed west to sight the new continent.
3. It happened because merchants wanted to establish trade routes using the seaway, rulers wanted to gain more power and wealth, people were curious about the world, new tools were available to help navigators on the seas.
4. It brought about many changes throughout the world: new crops, wealth, more trade, furs, horses, domesticated animals, diseases, and enslavement of Africans.
The story of Columbus has changed. We have more insights into the consequences of his discovery. Today, we are more concerned about human rights, and we note that human rights did not apply to non-Europeans during Columbus's time.

EXPLORATIONS IN THE NEW WORLD

Explorers and Their Accomplishments
          Page 13

1. M   8. F
2. E   9. A
3. K   10. C
4. B   11. L
5. I   12. H
6. J   13 N
7. D   14. G

What Makes a Great Explorer?   Page 14
1-4 Responses will vary.

THE IROQUOIS NATIONS– A CASE STUDY IN CULTURE

Studying Other American Indians   Page 18
The charts will vary.

Shawnee Chief, a Man of Peace   Page 19
1-3 Responses will vary.

EARLY SETTLEMENTS IN THE AMERICAS

Which Event Happened First?   Page 23
1. a   5. a
2. b   6. b
3. b   7. b
4. a   8. a

Nathaniel Bacon's Rebellion   Page 24
1. Responses will vary.
2. This incident is significant because it was the first revolt against an appointment of the king of England.

ENGLISH SETTLEMENTS IN NEW ENGLAND

Important People and Ideas   Page 23
1. D   7. C
2. I   8. A
3. G   9. H
4. L   10. K
5. J   11. E
6. B   12. F

Identifying the New England Colonies   Page 29
1. Map Study
2. Responses will vary.

MORE ENGLISH SETTLEMENTS IN THE NEW WORLD

Vertical Time Line   Page 33
1607	j	1642	l
1620	a/k	1649	f
1620	k/a	1664	i
1626	d	1670	b
1630	g	1682	c
1632	e	1732	h

Colonial Population Growth   Page 34
Students will make graphs. Responses will vary. The increasing birthrate, larger-sized families, as well as immigration should be mentioned.

THE COLONIAL ECONOMY

"Triangular" Trade–Rum, Slaves, and Sugar   Page 38
1. furs, fish, fruit
2. manufactured goods
3. rice, indigo, tobacco, and furs.
4. rum
5. sugar and molasses
6. slaves

Comparing Colonial Economy in the North and in the South   Page 39

Chart–The responses will vary

LIFE IN COLONIAL AMERICA

Witchcraft in the Colonies   Page 43
1. They supported the trials because they wanted their followers to obey the laws of the church.
2. Responses will vary.
3. Responses will vary.

Comparing Life in the North and in the South   Page 44
Responses will vary.

RIVALRY BETWEEN FRANCE AND ENGLAND IN THE NEW WORLD

The Acadians Page 48
1. He felt they were a threat because they refused to become British citizens and would support the French.
2. Responses will vary.
3. Responses will vary.

The French and Indian War Page 49
1-12 Responses will vary.

CHALLENGING BRITISH AUTHORITY

People and Events Page 53

1.	e	8.	f
2.	n	9.	l
3.	b	10.	m
4.	h	11.	a
5.	c	12.	g
6.	d	13.	j
7.	i	14.	k

What Does It Mean? Page 54

1.	e	6.	i
2.	a	7.	d
3.	g	8.	f
4.	b	9.	c
5.	j	10.	h

1. The Stamp Act and the Townshend Acts were repealed.
2. They refused to buy tea. The tea was dumped into the Boston harbor and the English lost money.
3. The Parliament could be compared to our Congress. Congress also has two bodies: the Senate and the House of Representatives.

THE WINNING OF INDEPENDENCE

Strengths and Weaknesses of Military Forces in the American Revolution Page 58
A few examples:
U.S. Strengths
    strongly committed soldiers
    assistance of French Navy and military leaders
    inspired by *Common Sense* and Declaration of Independence
    soldiers trained in fighting French and Indian War
U.S. Weaknesses
    most of the soldiers poorly trained and disciplined
    weak governmental structure to carry out a war
    shortage of military supplies and food
British Strengths
    strong, well-trained army and navy
    support of Loyalists
    strong leadership in government
    financial support for war
British Weaknesses
    weak military leaders
    lack of strong commitment to fight Americans
    lack of a military plan
1. & 2. Responses will vary.

Major Influences on American Thinking Page 59
Common Sense
    People should be free and independent.
    People should govern themselves.
    Governmental leaders should be selected on the basis of talent and not birth.
    Colonialism was cruel and unfair.

Declaration of Independence
    All men are created equal.
    All men are entitled to life, liberty, and the pursuit of happiness.
    Governments get their authority from the people.
    If a government does not meet the people's needs, the people have a right to destroy it.

BEGINNINGS OF A NEW NATION

The Constitution–Document of Freedom Page 63
1. Person should be 25 years old, 7 years a citizen of the United States, and elected in the state of residence.
2. Responses will vary.
3. Person should be a natural-born citizen of the United States, 35 years old, and a resident for 14 years of the United States. Responses will vary.
4. President has military powers, treaty-making, and appointive powers with the advice and consent of Congress. The president carries out the laws passed by Congress, receives representatives from foreign countries, and delivers a State of the Union message each year. Responses will vary.
5. The president appoints members of the Supreme Court who are competent and well-trained.
6. The Supreme Court interprets laws and treaties. The Chief Justice presides at impeachment hearings of the president.
7. *Checks and Balances* refers to the system of separation of powers among the legislative, executive, and judicial branches of government. Each operates independently but has a check on the other two.
8. This gives people in a free society the process through which changes can be made.

The Bill of Rights Page 64
Amendments 1-10. Responses will vary.
A. and B. Responses will vary.

LAUNCHING THE NEW GOVERNMENT

Which Event Happened First? Page 68

1.	b	6.	a
2.	a	7.	b
3.	b	8.	b
4.	a	9.	b
5.	b	10.	a

What Does It Mean? Page 69

1.	n	8.	i
2.	d	9.	c
3.	a	10.	k
4.	f	11.	m
5.	b	12.	h
6.	l	13	g
7.	j	14.	e

ERA OF JEFFERSONIAN POLICIES

The United States in 1804 Page 73
Map Study

National Censuses Page 74
Responses will vary.

CONFLICTS WITH THE BRITISH AND THE INDIANS

Dolley Madison, First Lady Page 78
Responses will vary.
1-5 Responses will vary.

People, Events, and Terms
Page 79

1. h		9. l	
2. i		10. d	
3. e		11. b	
4. k		12. n	
5. p		13. j	
6. o		14. f	
7. m		15. c	
8. g		16. a	

AMERICAN NATIONALISM AND SECTIONALISM

Influential Persons in Government
Page 83

1. f, i	6. c, r
2. d, q	7. e, o
3. g, s	8. a, m
4. k, t	9. j, p
5. b, l	10. h, n

Presidential Elections
Page 84

A. Responses will vary.
B. Responses will vary.
C. Responses will vary.

THE ERA OF JACKSONIAN DEMOCRACY

Reception for the People's President
Page 88

1. Responses will vary.
2. Responses will vary.

Identifying Nicknames
Page 89

1. b, h	6. g
2. e, f, j	7. a
3. i	
4. c, d	
5. k	

THE ABOLITIONISTS AND SLAVERY

Supporting and Abolishing Slavery in the 1850s
Page 93

Chart: the responses will vary.

    For: needed on plantations, necessary for economy
Against: one should not own another human being

Organizing Data
Page 94

A. 1, 2, and 4
    Line 1, free state
    Line 2, 1820
    Line 4, 1803
B. 1 and 4
    Line 1, act of freeing the slaves
    Line 4, stood for keeping slavery out of the territories
C. 3 and 4
    Line 3, *Narrative of the Life of Frederick Douglass*
    Line 4, *Uncle Tom's Cabin*

WESTWARD EXPANSION

Map Study
Page 98

Louisiana Purchase
Florida Cession
Texas Annexation
Mexican Cession
Oregon Country
Gadsden Purchase

Analyzing the Mexican War
Page 99

1. May 13, 1846
2. Mexico had refused to honor its financial obligations, insulted the United States by rejecting the Slidell mission, and had crossed the Rio Grande River and attacked American soldiers.
3. The Mexican and American governments as well as the Texans
4. The Mexican government wanted to exert its control by having its citizens obey its laws; the Texans wanted their independence from Mexico, and some people in the United States wanted more land.
5. The Mexicans lost the war; according to the treaty, United States acquired California and New Mexico, the southern boundary was acknowledged as the Rio Grande River. The United States agreed to assume claims of its citizens against Mexico and pay Mexico $15 million.
6. The responses will vary.

THE APPROACHING CRISIS OF DISUNION

People and Their Achievements
Page 103

1. g	6. i
2. f	7. h
3. d	8. a
4. e	9. c
5. j	10. b

Making Connections
Page 104

1. Henry Clay was the senator who studied all of the measures previously presented to the Senate and combined them into the Compromise of 1850. He introduced the compromise to the Senate. He was a strong advocate for compromise.
2. Stephen A. Douglas was a senator from Illinois who ran against Abraham Lincoln for reelection. While campaigning, they presented a number of debates on crucial national issues. Abraham Lincoln lost this election, but he won when he ran against Douglas for president of the United States.
3. John Brown led a group of men to Harper's Ferry and raided the federal arsenal. He was caught, found guilty, and sentenced to death by hanging. In the North he became a martyr and a hero for the cause of anti-slavery.
4. Because the Northerners were infuriated with the Fugitive Slave Act, they organized a system for helping escaped slaves reach freedom.
5. Cotton was the main cash crop for the South, a product which brought them prosperity and great wealth. Cotton needed laborers to work in the fields and this led to the demand for slaves to work on the plantations.
6. Daniel Webster and John C. Calhoun were both senators. Daniel Webster supported the anti-slavery view while John C. Calhoun supported the pro-slavery citizens. Both of the men were deeply committed citizens and excellent orators.
7. Roger Taney was the chief Justice in the Supreme Court who handed down the decision that blacks were not citizens; therefore, Dred Scott could not be treated as a "citizen" of the United States. He could not do those things which were guaranteed for citizens.
8. When the Kansas-Nebraska Act was passed, it permitted the two territories to decide by voting whether to become a free or a slave state. Northerners helped antislavery citizens move to those territories and resisted the enforcement of the Fugitive Slave Law. The voting was fraudulent. Towns were attacked and occasionally someone was killed. Then, the other group would organize for revenge. Five men were killed in one raid.